The Vates Anthology

of

New Latin Poetry

Edited by Mark Walker

Vates: The Journal of New Latin Poetry

is available for free download at

http://pineapplepubs.snazzystuff.co.uk/vates.htm

'ego Lar sum familiaris'

A *Pineapple Publications* Publication

First published 2015

Pineappple Publications

ISBN 978-0-9547473-4-3

Also from Pinepple Publications:

Amida: A Novel

More by Mark Walker

Annus Horribilis: Latin for Everyday Life (The History Press)

Annus Mirabilis: More Latin for Everyday Life (The History Press)

Britannica Latina: 2,000 Years of British Latin (The History Press)

Geoffrey of Monmouth's Life of Merlin: A New Verse Translation

(Amberley Publications)

Hobbitus Ille (HarperCollins)

Pineapple Publications

Contents

Introduction

This book is an entirely miscellaneous collection of new Latin poems written in the early years of the 21st century by a highly diverse group of poets whose shared passion for producing Latin poetry is their only unifying characteristic. Many are native English speakers, but quite a few are not: the community of Latin poets is genuinely international. The contributions are drawn predominantly from the pages of *Vates: The Journal of New Latin Poetry*, a free online publication founded in 2010 with the aim of providing a forum for the few remaining exponents of this venerable (and, yes, let's be honest, somewhat eccentric) art form – as well as to inspire new writers to try it for themselves.

I make no apology for the eclectic nature of either the journal or this book. Some of the contributors are professional academics, some are amateurs; some are experienced Latin poets, some are complete beginners. Some of the poems are translations of vernacular works; many are original pieces. Some are written in classical quantitative verse; some follow the rhythmic and rhyming poetry of medieval Latin; others are cast in moulds entirely new to Latin such as the haiku or the quincouplet; still others are in no particular metrical scheme at all.

Note that I use the words *poem* and *poetry* advisedly here and contrast them quite deliberately with *verse*. In issue #5 of *Vates*, Barry Baldwin introduced readers to a Victorian curiosity called the Eureka Machine, a lumbering proto-computer which, by means of an ingenious arrangement of cogs and wheels, was able to churn out perfect Latin hexameters on demand. It was all the rage in 1845 apparently. The lesson I take from the story of this clever contraption is that the ability to produce metrically correct Latin verse is decidedly *not* the same thing as being a Latin poet – for if it were, *reductio ad absurdum*, the Eureka Machine would have to be included in the pantheon of Neo-Latin poets alongside John Milton, Thomas Gray, Vincent Bourne and Walter Savage Landor *et al.*.

The Eureka Machine exemplifies one of the most powerful reasons for the decline in writing Latin poetry over the last ... well, the last few centuries really ... namely an increasingly pedantic over-emphasis on form over content – that is, on the external mechanics of Latin versifying to the detriment of the far more nebulous inner substance that makes a piece of verse a poem. In days gone by schoolchildren were drilled in the oft-dreaded 'verse comp', and any budding young Latin poet who dared to end a pentameter with anything other than a classic Ovidian disyllable lived in fear of being rapped over the knuckles by a disaproving schoolmaster (*Tom Brown's Schooldays* satirises the whole dispiriting procedure brilliantly). One of the unexpected benefits of the almost total disappearance of such lessons in schools is that modern Latin poets – most of whom are self-taught – are arguably less constrained than earlier generations when it comes to experimenting. Which is not to downplay the need for a clear understanding of matters metrical, especially when using the quantitative verse of the Roman poets, so long as we bear in mind that metrically sound *verse* is not *ipso facto* the same thing as a *poem*, and that this Anthology is concerned with *poetry* – even if each contributor here will have quite distinct ideas about what qualifies as poetry in the first place.

With every new issue of *Vates* new writers appear, many enthused by reading the contributions in previous issues. This is very encouraging – and I smugly tell myself that a small part of the reason is that, although I am in fact a schoolteacher by day, I am not in the habit of rapping anyone over the knuckles. All contributors to the journal are warmly welcomed. There are no restrictions. That's the whole point: to encourage anyone and everyone to have a go. Perhaps as a result the flame that once seemed all but extinguished is burning just a little brighter now.

The entries in this book are arranged alphabetically by author. Each entry follows the same format as that of the journal, with introductory comments from the poet followed by the Latin text and an English translation. When I began *Vates* I felt that the inclusion of translations would help make the poems seem a little less daunting, especially for amateur or beginning Latinists. Even though the panel of contributors has gradually expanded to include many more from non-English-speaking countries I still feel the English translations are useful for many readers who, while able to enjoy the wonderful sounds and rhythms of the Latin, may from time to time appreciate a little help.

All the contributors give their work to *Vates* freely, and the same is true for this Anthology. The time will probably never come when a Latin poet can expect any sort of financial reward – yes, we really do do it for love – but it is my hope that this little collection will give all of us who profess a wish to keep the ancient art alive some hope for the future.

Mark Walker

Carmina Latina

A note on spelling

Spelling and orthography follow that of the *Oxford Latin Dictionary*, hence no distinction is made between vocalic and consonantal 'i' and 'u', and only proper names are capitalised.

*   *   *

Lucis Alter

Lucius Alter lives in Santa Fe, New Mexico. He has been a restauranteur, and has taught *World Religions* and *Classical Languages*. He has also taught courses on planning and zoning issues and construction and design topics as they relate to community based low income housing development. He was a proposal writer for not-for-profit community organizations involved in poor peoples' housing and in ex-offender training and reintegration, and he did stints as a community organizer, an advocate for the homeless, and Director of Technical Services for New York City's now defunct Division of Homeless Housing Development.

4 Versiculi

Lucius writes: These are epigrams in elegiac couplets. The first is for a young man who was bound and beaten to death in a mental hospital. When I wrote it I had in mind some of the flower imagery found in the *Hymn to Demeter*, the emblematic character of violets as calming flowers, and the ancient myth of Persephone greeting the newly dead. The second is just the vagary of an undisciplined mind (mine) in the *Sangre De Cristo* range. The third was occasioned by the cremation of my sister-in-law at a monastery in Northern Thailand where I performed the duty of setting her body on fire and, the next morning, gathered her ashes and dropped them into the water off a sandbar near the triangulation of Burma, Thailand and Laos. The fourth is a reminiscence of a long dead lady who should not have died so young.

(1) Ad amicum Ricardum Vulpem qui in ualetudinario insanus est interfectus, a.d. V Kal. Feb. MMIII

> care mihi, dormi, neque flumine tu rediture,
>   detque tibi uiolas florida Persephone.

7

To Richard Fox, Who Was Murdered in a State Mental Hospital February 10, 2003

> Sleep, my dear friend, who will not cross the river,
> and may flower-fresh Persephone's violets be yours.

(2) De defectione Lunae

> *iunipero pendet uiridanti nigra Selene:*
> *stirpi sunt Cadmi cornua sicca cinis.*
> *iunipero pendet uiridanti nigra Selene:*
> *noctua contristans carmina maesta canit.*

Eclipse of the Moon

> Above the verdant junipers a black
> moon hangs. Actaeon's antlers are dry ash.
> Above the verdant junipers a black
> moon hangs. The sorrowful owl mourns in song.

(3) Cineres in uento

> *optima, ne maneas: patiaris spiritus aeque*
> *consurgat uentis quam cinis alba tibi.*

To the Ghost of my Sister-in-Law

> Dearest, do not linger. Like your pale
> ashes, may your soul rise up on the wind.

(4) Nullo titulo

> *tu quoque mortalis, quondam nigra fecerat ouum*
> *muscula mellitis basiolisque tuis.*

Untitled

> You too were born to die, for once a small,
> dark fly laid its eggs in the honey of your kisses.

Metre: Elegiacs

*   *   *

Three Poems

Lucius writes: I am very fond of crickets and of the *Palatine Anthology*, both of which inspired the first poem. One day as I was sweeping the bricks around my fireplace, I accidentally bludgeoned an unfortunate cricket who had strayed out of the wood pile. The poem is the bugslaughter's aftermath, an elegiac *wergild* of sorts. The second poem concerns Bub, a white wolf hybrid who was very strong, but gentle and loyal. Like Mithridates, he died old. The third is dedicated to Edward, a fine, humane fellow with whom, from time to time, I have corresponded. I would not have chosen the tone and vocabulary of this piece if I didn't like and respect him, and I am certain he was no more offended by it when I sent it to him some time ago than I have been by his often frank remarks.

(1) De Morte Praematura Violentaque Achetae Domesticae

> ex pauimento te moui, mi paruule grille,
>   protinus ad Ditis litora maesta dei.
> carmina per fuscos calamos industria fundis
>   tristibus ad ripas has Acherontis aquae.
> stant nullo nummo manibus tendentibus umbrae
>   vitis tunc raptis nunc animisque suis.
> sunt inopes, errant, et eunt in tristibus oris,
>   sub terras virides, carceribusque suis.
> Cerberus, iste canis, tenet ostia ferrea dirus
>   Lethes dum sperant aequora traiiciant.
> grillule, tu naui latitans conderis amictu,
>   et tunc invisus mortua traiicies.
> ingredieris per portas Acherontis auari
>   quo domini maneas Ditis in aede sacra.

On the Untimely and Violent Death of Acheta Domestica

> Little cricket, I swept you from my floor
> Clear to the edge of Hades' sombre shore,
> Where, crouched among the murky reeds, you sing
> A busy tune for those mirthless souls who ring
> The thick, paludal ripe of River Styx.
> Destitute they stand, a pallid mix
> Of outstretched arms and spent mortality.
> Cast out from an arid maw of penury,
> They do hard time: a hundred years they'll wait
> To dare the dog and the adamantine gate.
> But you, little cricket, will stow a ride
> To the black River of Death's other side,
> Where, in the fold of a chiton, you'll slip
> Unnoticed into Hades' final keep.

(2) Ad Bub, Candidum Lupum-Canem Qui XV Annos Natus Amnem Traiecit

ne iam plumbosi mingas, lupe, Ditis in atrum
cerbereumque canem triplicem qui ringitur asper.
frenduntur dentes, sequitur, seruitque seueris
diuis: purpureas subter uiolas Rhadamanthi
sceptrum tu teneas inter labra: prataque crure
alte sublato laetantia mox madefiant.

To Bub, a White Wolf Hybrid Who Died at Age Fifteen

Wolf, do not piss on three headed Cerberus,
the black, fierce, growling dog of leaden Dis.
Obedient, he gnashes his teeth in the service
of harsh gods: under the purple violets
may you hold in your jaws Rhadamanthus'
sceptre, and with your bent leg lifted high,
may you moisten his flowering meadows.

(3) Hendecasyllabi ad Eduardum epistularum scriptorem

Eduarde optime, mi sodalis Arge,
pusulas natibus meis rubellas
quare tam uehementer indolescis?
cuique spongia nonne stercoratur?

Hendecasyllables for Edward the Letter Writer

Edward, my dear fellow, ever watchful,
why do you persist in lavishing attention
on all the red pimples that cover my ass?
Who is there whose toilet paper's not covered with shit?

Metres: Elegiacs (1), Hexameters (2), Hendecasyllables (3)

*   *   *

Ocelli Virides

Lucius writes: Just an informational note on *smaragdis:* in Martial 5.11.1 the *a* in the second syllable is light: *Sardonychas, zmaragdos, adamantas, iaspidas uno...*

Sarcion est tibi nil minime, gratissima domna,
fulgenti smaragdis luminibusque tuis.

10

Metre: Elegiacs

Translation: *Green Eyes*

 Dearest lady, there is no cloud or flaw in you,
  And in your flashing eyes green fire shines true.

* * *

XLIV Magnum

Lucius writes: These hasty, merry little hendecasyllables spring from that well of rollicking, irrepressible optimism which is my soul.

 hoc plumbum inspicias, amice, paruum
 quod mihi minimum uidetur esse,
 etsi sufficit ut cere uacet brum
 plumbo iam fatuum meummet isto.

Metre: Hendecasyllables

Translation: *44 Magnum*

 Look at this little piece of lead.
 It doesn't seem like very much.
 Yet I think it's quite enough
 To empty out my silly head.

* * *

Ante Diem X Kalendas Decembres
MMDCCLXVI A.U.C.

Lucius writes: A short epigram. Note that *illudere* = *illusio* = *ironia*.

 iudicio facto peiorum illudere magnum est,
  historiae quamquam iam quibus actus erit.

Metre: Elegiacs

Translation: *November 22, 2013.*

 Judgments of lesser men are irony,
 Though there are some will call it history.

* * *

Lydia Ariminensis

Lydia Ariminensis is the Latin nickname of Lidia Brighi, graduate and specialized with a two year master in Classical Letters at the Università di Bologna (Italy). She teaches letters, Latin and Greek at the Liceo ginnasio Giulio Cesare in Rimini. She writes regularly articles and poems in Latin for the web magazine *Ephemeris* http://ephemeris.alcuinus.net/index.php and she is part of editorial board of the monthly magazine of crosswords and puzzles in Latin *Hebdomada Aenigmatumm* http://www.mylatinlover.it/italian_2.html. She obtained a *publica laus* in the *Certamen Scevola Mariotti* , the acknowledgements of which were given in April 2013 at the Università Pontificia Salesiana, Rome.

De Discipulorum Reditu Ab Otio Aestivo

Lydia writes: I wrote this short poem in autumn 2013, thinking of the mood of many students who, coming back to school without enthusiasm, long for the summer amusements on the beach of Rimini and for the fellowship of friends, many of whom live far away.

aestas autumno cedit uario nebulisque
    cuncta albent fusis, pallida humi folia
in strata crepitant saeuo cumuli pede fracti
    ui uentus magna fert spolia arborea
sub Foebo tenui uoluuntur uortice torto
    paruo circuitu peruolitant leuiter:
ut studiis pueri se dent maesti reuocantur.
    otia dimittunt, laetitiae comites
- sol et litora amoena aer feruensque ualete!-
    lintres et cumbae limine in aequoreo
non lusus laeto resonant clamore iocique
    non ardens splendet litus apud pelagus,
orae incultae adstant peregrinis aere fusco:
    hic illic rari conspiciunt abeunt
sub pluuia risus pulchras memorantque puellas
    quas alias alio cura paterna refert.
discipuli redeunt ad munus tempore dato
    emptum concurrunt en tabulas calamos
libros et peras - dulces coetus ualeatis ! -
    ecce magistri illis ardua munera dant
- Vergilius docet - at labor improbus omnia uincit
    dummodo continuo dent operam adsiduam
dum redeat iucunda aestas omnesque cachinni!

Metre: Elegiacs

Translation: *The Return of Students from their Summer Holidays*

Summer gives place to colourful autumn and everything is white for the spreading mist, pale leaves crackle on the ground on the street, heaps crashed with cruel feet, the wind carries away tree spoils with great strength, under the week sunshine they whirl with circular eddies, fly here and there gently drawing small turns. Boys, in a sad mood, are recalled to their studies. They leave leisure, fellow of joy. 'Sun and pleasant beaches and hot weather, farewell!' On the seaside boats do not echo anymore for funny screams of jokes and games, the scorching beach does not shine anymore next to the sea, wild shores lay in front of travellers under a cloudy sky: here and there few of them look around and go away under the rain, remembering laughters and nice girls, whom the care of their fathers brought back to different places. For the present, students go back to their duty, they crowd to buy notebooks, pens, books and sacks. Farewell, sweet companies! Look, teachers assign hard homeworks to them - Vergil says - but hard work wins everything, as long as they work continually and assiduously, until funny summer and all laughters come back!

*　　*　　*

De Instantibus Hominibus Curis

Lydia writes: I drew my inspiration from some verses of the *Aeneid* (IV, vv. 522-532), which I read to my students with metrical rhythm:

Nox erat et placidum carpebant fessa soporem
corpora per terras, silvaeque et saeva quierant
aequora, cum medio volvuntur sidera lapsu,
cum tacet omnis ager, pecudes pictaeque volucres,
quaeque lacus late liquidos quaeque aspera dumis
rura tenent, somno positae sub nocte silenti.
[lenibant curas et corda oblita laborum.]
at non infelix animi Phoenissa, neque umquam
solvitur in somnos oculisve aut pectore noctem
accipit: ingeminant curae rursusque resurgens
saevit amor magnoque irarum fluctuat aestu.

I remembered the famous night poem of Alcman too (Fr. 89P):

εὕδουσι δ᾽ ὀρέων κορυφαί τε καὶ φάραγγες
πρώονές τε καὶ χαράδραι
φῦλά τ᾽ ἑρπέτ᾽ ὅσα τρέφει μέλαινα γαῖα
θῆρές τ᾽ ὀρεσκώιοι καὶ γένος μελισσᾶν
καὶ κνώδαλ᾽ ἐν βένθεσσι πορφυρέας ἁλός·
εὕδουσι δ᾽ οἰωνῶν φῦλα τανυπτερύγων.

Recalling to my mind these renowned verses, I composed something fitting to our times.

13

nox est, astra micant placido labentia caelo
sed nobis dehinc e luce minore tremescunt
urbis in aere conspectu fusco nebuloso,
ante tabernas cauponasque ubicumque domorum
lumine fuso, nec somnus mortalibus aegris
nocte ob clamorem tota conceditur ullus.
multi tam cupidi quaestus quocumque uagantur
solliciti numquam quod captum sit satis illis
se raroque solent consumpti dare quieti.
sunt qui continuo morbis miseri crucientur
quique carentes extollant palmas inopesque
cum uiuendi non illis spes ulla decore
nec dormire licet nisi sub Diuo iacituri.
dormit dura ferarum stirps, ac stant ut inertes
aerii uolucres in ramis immemoresque
lassa manent insecta cauernis clam colubrique
tradunt sese domi feles catulique sopori
non requiescit gens uigilans hominum miserorum
curis et fato uexatur nocte dieque

Metre: Hexameters

Translation: *Worries Oppressing People*

It is night, fading stars are shining in the quiet sky, but for us beneath they tremble with dim light in the foggy air of the town, confused to the sight, as plenty of light spreads in front of hotels and bars and houses and no sleep is allowed to weary people throughout the night because of noise.

Many people craving for gain wander here and there anxiously, because they have never got enough and seldom retire. Others are tortured unceasingly with diseases, others lift up their hands in their poverty, as they have no hope of a dignified life and cannot sleep but in the open.

The hard progeny of wild beasts is sleeping, birds of the air lie like dead and forgetful on branches, weary bugs and snakes remain hidden in caves, cats and dogs fall asleep at home. But the progeny of unhappy men does not rest because of worries and is vexed by the fate all day and night long.

*   *   *

Barry Baldwin

Barry Baldwin was born a true 'Lincolnshire Yellowbelly', but emigrated first to Australia, thence to Canada, where he is Emeritus Professor of Classics (University of Calgary) and a Fellow of the Royal Society of Canada. He has published 12 books and c.1000 articles/reviews *apropos* Greek, Roman and Byzantine history and literature, Neo-Latin Poetry, Samuel Johnson, Modern English Literature, and the more arcane field of Albanian history, language and literature. Has also published c.70 short stories, mainly mysteries, and freelances on a farrago of subjects for various magazines. He is a regular contriobutor of articles to *Vates*. He remains a far-off fan of Lincoln City and Nottingham Forest.

Aue, Vates

Barry Baldwin writes: A little something to hail *Vates*. It is framed by opening and closing lines from Propertius and Martial.

> cedite, Romani scriptores; cedite, Grai!
> advenit – en! – VATES, docti super aegide Marci.
> advenit – en! – VATES, idcirco gaudeat omnis
> qui cupiat versus edendos scribere Marco.
> Hispani memini verissima verba poetae:
> sint Maecenates, non derunt, Marce, Marones!

Metre: Hexameters

Translation:

> Make way Roman writers, make way, Greeks! See! *Vates* has arrived, under the aegis of learned Mark. See! *Vates* has arrived, so let all rejoice who desire to write verses for publication by Marcus. I remember the wise words of the Spanish poet: Let there be Maecenases, Mark, and Virgils will not be wanting!

*   *   *

Pete Bibby

Pete Bibby is retired and has returned to his Latin studies after a brief gap of 46 years.

In Senectute

Pete writes: I have always had a fondness for haiku and returning to my Latin studies after a brief gap of 46 years I was delighted to come across *Tonight They All Dance*. A latin haiku had to follow, so here is my first one.

> *in senectute,*
> *pulchrae fiunt pulchriores;*
> *senex maneo.*

Metre: Haiku

Translation:

> In old age beautiful (women) become more beautiful (but) I remain an old man.

*   *   *

Stephen Coombs

Stephen Coombs was born in Weymouth on the English south coast in 1943 and studied Music at Balliol College, Oxford. Soon after graduating he moved to Stockholm and taught music there. Languages, not least Latin, have been among his abiding interests. In 1994 he co-founded a free school in Uppsala where in defiance of educational fashion he was able to include an introductory Latin course in the syllabus. He retired from teaching in 2010.

In Perendinum Aevum

Stephen writes: The four poems I have chosen for this anthology are contained in my collection of Latin poetry *In Perendinum Aevum* (Evertype http://www.evertype.com/books/in-perendinum-aevum.html). The first, *Puer* ('A Boy'), opens a group of pieces entitled *Vox Ter Cupida* ('Thrice Yearning Voice') set in the mouths of marginal figures mentioned in the Gospels. This is the boy with the loaves and fishes of John vi 8-13. With references to the Lord's Prayer and two parables (Matt. vi 12; xxv 14, 15, 27; xxii 19-21) he considers quite simply what is entailed by our human responsibility to be co-creators with God. The metrical pattern is the Second Pythiambic (cf. Horace's Epode xvi), dactylic hexameters alternating with (pure) iambic trimeters.

The other poems have novel metrical structures. *Ad Tibicinem* ('To a Clarinettist') is taken from a series called *Fragmenta Mythica* ('Mythic Fragments') where four kinds of 11-syllable verse are used in rotation: a Lesser Sapphic, a standard Hendecasyllabic or Phalaecean, this being in fact a re-arrangement of the feet of the Lesser Sapphic, a further such re-arrangement ('Mixophalaecean' – two trochees, spondee, dactyl and final trochee or spondee), and an iambic trimeter catalectic.

Diursolmiae ('In Djursholm') is the first of three *Extemporalia Ante Ver Inceptum* ('Pre-Spring Improvisations'). The strophe consists of a Mixophalaecean, two iambic trimeters catalectic and half an elegiac pentameter, i.e. two dactyls (of which the former is here allowed to be replaced by a spondee) and a final extra syllable. Successful artistic designs combine homogeneity and heterogeneity. In the strophe of *De Non Haesitante Amore Meditatio Vespertina* ('Unhesitating Love: an Evening Meditation') the opening syllable sequence common to the Lesser Asclepiadean (in the second verse) and the Hendecasyllabic/Phalaecean (in the third) is also applied to the dactylic hexameter of the first verse and the Greater Sapphic of the fourth.

Puer

> reddere quae nequeo, potero quae soluere nunquam
> rogo remitte mille magna debita:
> at quae pauca fero tamen accipe paupera dona:
> inopsne saccus hordeaceos habet
>
> quinque manu matris panes super igne paratos
> (recepit omne partus a parentibus)

17

atque duos pisces correptos rete paterno?
et ecquid inde multitudinem beet?

nil turbae dedo, tibi soli traditur esca:
trahatur in superna digna te loca.
sicut homo peregre proficiscens uiua ministro
talenta, quanta nescioue qualia,

respiciens proprias uires augenda dedisti.
pecunia arte nummularii lucrum
obtinet: arte tua, precor, auge credita seruo:
quid adferamus ante te nisi ex tuo?

cui nisi Christe tibi tradamus nostra talenta?
tuam nomisma iactat hic imaginem.
me trado tibi, me panem piscemque creanti:
fac ipse maius escam et indolem meam.

distribue acceptos panes, o diuide pisces,
sed haud edenda frusta frugis editae
restituas ne quid pereat pereamue relictus:
tuere Christe me uirentem et integrum.

Translation:

Remit, I pray, the thousand great debts which I cannot pay back and which I will never be able to discharge; but accept nonetheless the few poor gifts I bear; is it a worthless bag that holds five barley loaves prepared over the fire by my mother's hand - the offspring has received everything from its parents - and two fishes seized in my father's net? And can any of this be a blessing to the multitude? I surrender nothing to the crowd, the food is handed to you alone: may it be drawn into realms above that are worthy of you.   Like a man leaving on a journey you have given your servant with regard to his strengths living talents to be augmented in value, I know not how great or of what sort. Money acquires profit by the art of the money-lender; increase, I beg, by your art what has been entrusted to your servant, for what can we bring before you unless it be from what is yours? To whom, if not to you, Christ, should we make over our talents? It is your image the coin here boasts! I hand myself over to you, bread and fish to you who created me: be yourself the maker of something more from my food and my innate potential. Accept and distribute the loaves, oh share out the fishes, but restore the crumbs that are not to be consumed of the produce given out, lest anything be lost, or lest I be left behind and lost; O Christ, keep me safe, thriving and whole.

*   *   *

Ad Tibicinem

mel meum, si caecus amicus essem
  tunc ferres mihi opem: libente clemens
    mente cogitansque abscondita uenis
      deflectereris ut tuam tenebris
tangerem dulcem faciem. negabis
  non fracto calamoue arundiniue
    gratiam intimam: caedine opus esset
      fortasse formarique iam priore
sorte quassato mihi ut ore dignus
  mellito fierem? uide cruentum
    cor doloris hic rasum mihi cultro!
      uidens tamen non flecteris uidenti.

Translation:

My love, if I were a blind friend, then you would come to my aid; willingly merciful in your mind and thinking secrets in your veins you would bend down so that I might touch your sweet face in the darkness. You will deny intimate favour to a reed or rush that has not been broken; already shaken by an earlier fate, might I perhaps need now to be cut and shaped so as to be made worthy your honeyed mouth? See here my bloody heart, scraped by sorrow's knife! But you seeing do not bend for me seeing.

*   *   *

Diursolmiae

paginas libri scripturus apertas
  quondam tenebam: nonne iam recludi
    debent legendae? uere uerum agetur,
      uer reserandum ineo.

sunt aquae freti crateris imago
  turba colorum picta caerulorum:
    dulcem gulae salsamque mattearum
      uimque refert acidam.

his aquis dedit Germania nomen:
  Horatiine caerula illa pubes
    bellata belua atque bella epodo
      in sexto decimo,

seu color uitro debetur agresti
      seu luminum splendore noscitatur
      seu sicut a pictore Geinsboroeo
        in tabula pueri

elegantia tentatur amictus,
      ueram domum unam fluctibus Boreis
      habet sinus quem saepe uisitaui,
      hic modo ubi sedeo?

saepe caerulus signum color edit
      haud esculentorum cibariorum:
      caelo pericla praemonemur ipso
        atque liquente mari.

tot tamen diu res sunt uetitae uel
      et nunc uetantur: nonne sit necesse
      contemnere interdicta longa? quando
        rex nisi nunc fierem?

nonne iam mihi sors suscipiatur?
      quae scripseram ante hunc saeculi quadrantem,
      cum credere ausus non eram notari
        mi dictata alio

sed putaueram tracta esse meamet
      ex cogitatione, uerba prompsi
      antiqua iudex si liceret aequus
        ut legerem senior.

digna adest quies. desiderat aulam
      silere ueritatis explicator,
      hortatur hortum et uer silere siluam
        crescat ut omne nouum.

digna adest quies. uult firma patrari
      pax ante uer, pax ante ueritatem.
      placet sedere hic ante codicem artis
        quae latet intus adhuc.

continet crucis multum diagramma
      croci colore et tulipae libellus.
      quam prisca oblectat pax, nec ipsa uera

nec fallax, animam
uere nec manumissam nec apertam!
  post septuagenarium gerendi
    tempus quod illustre et queat stupendum
      nobile grande pari!

fluctuum fit aequor caeruleorum
  complexio perfusa, muscus autem
    fusco uiret colore tamquam oliuae
      quas nube umbra tegit:

glaucus aspero lichen superauit
  pallore saxum: sed freti uidete
    perfectionem congerentem aceruo
      sapphiros uarios:

cur petam colorum ollas aliorum?
  uel cur libellus debeat recludi?
    fortasse non necesse uindicare est
      quae promissa habui:

namque conditur photone oculum omni
  pellente partus floreae procellae:
    denos abhinc iam sexies duobus
      annos sepositis

uastitate in Eoa lapicidae
  Portlandiensis florui citatus
    lichene flauo candidaque rupe
      aestate et calida:

rupibus marinis et mihi quid sit?
  prudenter hoc sat dicerem mare esse
    etsi frequentatum insulis minutis
      ac domitum breuibus.

insulae uiatorem impediuntque
  me notiones desidem insolentes:
    suffocor altitudine aestuum aegre
      sufficiente animae:

at creatio, diuina poësis,
  inest inaudita atque operta cordi.

*futura uates non canam: loquar quae
tempora iam tulerint.*

Translation: *In Djursholm*

I used to hold the book's pages open to write - oughtn't they now to be
opened to be read? In spring the truth shall be dealt with. I enter spring to
unlock it.   The waters of this channel are the image of a bowl painted in
a myriad of blues, bringing the gullet a power of tasty morsels, sweet, salt
and sour. Germania has given this water its name: that blue youngsterdom
of Horace, a monster but handsome warring in the sixteenth epode - be the
colour due to the woad of the fields or noted in the splendour of eyes or put
to the test in choiceness of clothing as by the painter Gainsborough in his
picture of a boy - has that youngsterdom for its one true home this bay of
the northern seas which I have visited often, where I am sitting at this very
moment? An azure colour often sends out a sign that what we might want
to eat should not be eaten; heaven itself warns us of danger and so does the
flowing sea. But so many things have been or are still forbidden; may it not
be time to defy long-standing prohibitions? When am I to be king if not
now? Shan't I take my fate upon myself? What I'd written a quarter of a
century before not daring to believe I was taking down another's dictation,
but thinking it all my own invention - these words from the past I've
disinterred to read them as an older man, if possible as an impartial judge.
It's good and quiet here. The unfolder of truth requires the lecture hall to be
silent, spring tells the garden and the woods to be silent so that all may
grow anew. It's good and quiet here. Determined to be established is peace
before spring, peace before truth. It is pleasant to sit here in front of the
book of an art still unrevealed inside.   Many a diagram of the cross in
the hues of crocus and tulip is contained by the little book. How pleasant
the primordial peace, neither true nor false, to a soul that in the spring is
unemancipated and unopened! After seventy years of gestation what an
illustrious,   stupendous, grand and majestic something may be brought
forth! The surface of the water becomes a saturated complexity of blue
ripples, while the moss has a dull green colour like that of olives overlaid
with a shadow of cloud; the glaucous lichen with its roughened pallor has
conquered the stone; but look at the perfection of the waters heaping
together a motley of sapphires; why should I seek vessels of other colours?
And why should the book necessarily be opened? Perhaps there's no need to
claim what I've been promised; for it's implicit in every photon that strikes
the eye that a storm of blossom will burst forth; it was as much as fifty-
eight years ago on the East Weares, a wilderness to Portland's quarrymen,
that I freshly bloomed, aroused by yellow lichen and bright white stone and
a hot summer; what is it with me and seaside rocks ? This I might
reasonably describe as sea, even though it's stuffed with tiny islands and
tamed by shallows.   The traveller's hindered by islands and I though
inactive by unconventional ideas, I'm choked by the depth of the waves
being hardly sufficient for my soul, but creation, divine productivity, is
contained unheard and hidden in my heart. With sacred voice I shan't
prophesy things to come, but speak of what time has already brought.

*   *   *

22

De Non Haesitante Amore Meditatio Vespertina

tellurem ipse deus factam contentus amauit:
dilexi ueniens officia inscius
coetus Oxoniensis orthodoxi:
sed nunc tam grauibus mihi casibus haud placet studere.

formosissima erant peperit quae diua potestas,
ac formam cecini saepe poematis,
quae si compta putet legique digna
ante aut post obitum discerpserit aula litterarum,

quae (si uaticiner) mea carmina grata gradatim
cunctanter statuet, namque habiles parum
scripturae modice nouae uidentur.
me ualde iuuenem modo Horatius afficit pauore

cuius uix operas trepidans aperire cupiui.
tollo forte librum, pagina mox patet,
ignota aspicio soluta uerba
quae sunt "nox erat et caelo" uelut antea repulsus

sim de proposita porta sine cardine Flacci
iamque admissus habens aduena tesseram:
pugno pignus inest, uocatus ergo
degustare queo tot cetera quot creauit ille.

me tam discipulus quam solus in arte magister
passus difficiles ac faciles dies
ludo confiteor datum libenter,
in quo paene fui uitam puer atque adultus omnem:

ast in principio, flens natus quattuor annos
insolabiter stratus in angulo
conclauis domina Coqua domati,
nequaquam potui me dicere iam scholas amare.

exemplum melius nihilum cessantis amoris
quaeratur. publicae plurima sunt rei,
cum ludis etiam, domi Boreae
quae temeta timet temeraria, potuum tabernae.

Sollentunam habitans capiti prope finitimam urbem
ostendit uegetus pegmate uenditor
potum quem licuit iubere tantum
mitti, legitime quem conderet inuehens petendum.

23

poenas ille tulit cepique ego praemia, pressa
a Turrensibus, hoc nomine Hiberico,
dein stillata duo et retenta lustra.
potus fortuito qui praebitus egit experiri

in lingua cubitans careo dulcedine raro
laute multiplici, ceu comite ilico
adsumpta liquida semel reperta.
quis non uult comitem, solamine quis negat iuuari?

quae de principio non sint permissa sinantur
edictis propriis. indicium mihi
factum Tonius est fidele Caupo,
fabellam expositus Thoma puer incohante Manno.

tanta huic mollitia est quanta huic ob lumina forma.
qua re non etiam ius mihi ducere
cessum mollitiae queam uidenti
magnam in qua facie, quo corpore pulchritudinem esse?

sensim suetus ut ille adulescens uiuere adulans
octauo Lubecum nactus eram die
Septembris peregrinus at per annos
uiginti placito quasi numine tractus huc et unum.

quam nunc pelliculam praebent ambobus ocellis
Scaenae Lucis, ita est uox, Capitolii?
uidi Tonium amiculumque terra
pigmento uiduos ubi dixerat auctor obuenire.

mens procedit ab his in pulchram agilemque figuram
raedarum statione historia probae
uisam Vintoniae. globus docendus
nobis captus erat parili prius inuicem relicto

interque aëroportum et Vimutiense uehebat
litus laophorum turbam alacerrimam.
aestas tertia post iter calebat
cui culmen Lubeci. mora commoda nunc erat tributa

cursus dimidio completo. laophorum omnes
euasere breui tempore. nunquam ero
oblitus gracilis leuis figurae
tam munda specie, tam nobilis ac salubris ore,

sustentae manibus positis in partibus altis
crebrorum iuueni gente sedilium,

24

conantis uacuum ad suum redire,
obstructo pedibus male tramite sarcinarum aceruis.

perpaulum potui cognoscere carne figuram:
palmis ac digitis. uix patria mea
illi saepe subinde sum locutus
et posthac etiam minus incola regiae Boreae,

sed sicut lapis e fornace ab origine lapsus
Vulcani (Veneri non propior fui)
crystallo memori tenente testor:
huc magneticam acum conuerterat intimus Cupido!

prompte nectar ades semper sanare paratum
nec frustratum hilaras spes miseri uiri.
te substantia saxea ordinata
membrorum bibat ut iaceat cito laxa. somnus instet.

Translation: *Unhesitating Love: an Evening Meditation*

Having made the world God himself was content and loved it; dear to me coming in ignorance were the rites of the Orthodox community living in Oxford; but now I don't choose to dwell on such weighty cases. Most beautiful was what power divine gave birth to, and I've often sung praise of beauty in my poems, which before or after my death the court of letters will tear to bits if they think them well-made and worth reading, but only deem pleasant (if I as a bard may prophesy) step by step, sluggishly - writing that's somewhat new seeming rather intractable. In my early youth it happens to be just Horace that strikes me with dread, and I've hardly yearned, in my trembling, to open his works. I pick up a book by chance, a page is soon visible, I spy these free-flowing, new to me words: "It was night and up in the sky" - as if I've been hitherto thrust away from Horace's hingeless confronting door, but admitted now that I turn up with a ticket; the key-card is in my fist, I'm therefore invited to taste and enjoy all the rest of what he has created. As a pupil and as a teacher alone at my job having known days both of ease and of difficulty, I confess myself willingly given over to school, where adult and child I've spent nearly all my life; though at the beginning in inconsolable tears just four years old, and lying prostrate in a corner of a room that was held in check by a lady called Cook, in no way could I declare I loved education. Let's look for a better example of love that will not delay. The state takes on lots of things, not only schools but moreover, in this northern land that's afraid of dangerous hard drink, liquor shops. A wide-awake salesman living in Sollentuna, a town not far from the capital, showed on his shelves a drink that was only allowed to be sent for, which by law its importer should store until it was asked for. He received punishment, I was rewarded with something Torres had pressed, that Iberian firm of renown, then distilled and withheld for a decade. The drink that was on offer by chance and got me to give it a try has a finely complex sweetness I rarely lack on my tongue when I go to bed, that once found I took straightaway as a liquid companion. Who'd not like a companion, who'd not choose to enjoy some comfort? Behaviour forbidden on principle may be allowed by special edict. For me it was Tonio Kröger that gave a reliable proof of this - the boy portrayed by Thomas Mann at the start of the story. His sensitiveness is just as great as the beauty before his eyes. Why

25

mightn't I draw the conclusion that I too was granted the right to be sensitive seeing great beauty in some face, some body? Having grown used to living, like that youth, an adorer, on the eighth of September I had arrived in Lübeck on my travels, but as if I'd been drawn there over the course of twenty-one years by a favouring godhead. What film are the Capitol-Lichtspiele (that's the name) presenting now to one's couple of eyes? I saw Tonio and his particular friend in black and white in the place where the author had said they met. My thoughts move on to the lithe and beautiful figure I saw in a car-park in historical Winchester. We had fetched a group we were going to teach, having turn and turn about taken leave of a similar one, and a coach was transporting between the airport and Weymouth's seaside a very lively crowd. The third summer after the journey that peaked in Lübeck was glowing. The drive being half completed now a welcome pause had been granted. Everyone briefly escaped the coach. I shall never forget that slender, nimble figure, so clean and neat in appearance, with a countenance of such wholesomeness and nobility, supported by hands that were placed on the tops of seats packed with young folk as it strove to return to its own empty one, since as far as feet were concerned the way was sorely obstructed by piles of luggage. In the flesh I got to know the figure but slightly - in palms and fingers. From then on I hardly spoke often to it where I was born, and even less frequently later housed in the northern royal city, but like a rock that had formed after oozing out of the forge of Vulcan (I've not got closer to Venus) I witness through crystals retentive in memory: here is where inner Desire had turned the magnetic needle! Come pronto, you nectar always prepared to bring healing, that's not betrayed a wretched man's cheerful hopes. May the stony, orderly substance of limbs absorb you and soon lie relaxed. It is time for sleep to pursue me.

*   *   *

Marco Cristini

Marco Cristini was born in 1992 in Brescia, Northern Italy (*Brixia Veronae mater amata meae*, CATULLUS, *Carmen LXVII*, 34; 60 km far from Virgil's Mantua). He studies Literature at the Catholic University of Brescia. He loves reading Latin poetry and prose since high school. In 2013 he fell under the charming spell of *Latinitas perennis* and began to write Latin poems, articles and short stories. He investigated the Latin Literature during the First World War, finding hundreds of (mostly very well-written) *carmina* and texts. He is also interested in Late Antiquity (as his poems show...), especially in the Ostrogothic Kingdom of Italy. He has written a novel about the queen Amalasuntha and Cassiodorus (*I Cavalieri del Crepuscolo*, *The Twilight's Knights*, available as an ebook).

Aetas Anxietatis

Marco writes: I wrote *Aetas Anxietatis* in August 2013 while thinking about the political and economical situation of Europe.

> *haec est aetas anxietatis,*
> *desperamus ciuitatis*
> *de salute crisi magna.*
> *spem occultant lata stagna*
> *nostrorum desiderorum*
> *tardo passu confectorum.*
> *mundus fit repente grauis,*
> *prodest uiris factis cauis*
> *non iam Atlas, non Augustus.*
> *animus horret angustus,*
> *mox posteritatis metus*
> *clam amabit homo uetus,*
> *spes quod sunt multae memoriae*
> *nam felicitatum gloriae.*
> *sed nunc quaero, quod futurum,*
> *quod cras aeuum est uenturum?*
> *iuuenes reperientne*
> *opus an aperientne*
> *desperationi portas?*
> *nubes nigras tum exortas*
> *specto magno cum timore*
> *illis nec credo clamore*
> *qui proclamant finem crisis.*

rebus publicis diuisis
Europaea fit mox clades,
nox extremas inter Gades
et litteratas Athenas.
non frangemus has catenas
Europa ni fit unita,
aeuo nouo permunita.

Metre: Rhythmic

Translation: *The Age of Anxiety*

> This is the age of anxiety,
> we despair of the state's fate
> because of the big crisis.
> Hope is hidden by
> the wide ponds of our desires
> dead with terrible slowness.
> The world becomes suddenly heavy,
> helps the men turned empty
> not Atlas, not Augustus.
> The narrow soul horrifies,
> soon the old man will secretly
> love future's fear,
> because hopes are lots of memories
> of the happiness' glory.
> But now I ask, what future,
> what age is coming tomorrow?
> Young people will find
> a job or they'll open
> the doors to despair?
> I look at black clouds recently appeared
> with great worry
> and I don't trust those who with outcry
> say that the crisis is over.
> Because nations are divided
> there will be soon a big European defeat,
> a night between the extreme Gades
> and the learned Athens.
> We will not break these chains,
> unless Europe is truly united,
> fortified for a new age.

*   *   *

Niuis Mundus/Mundos

Marco writes: This is an experimental work, but I hope it might awake some Latin enthusiast's interest in Old Latin. In 2012 I attended a university course on Old Latin Grammar. It is a very interesting subject; almost everyone who studies Latin sometimes struggles with 'strange' exceptions, as *pater familias*, *fructubus* (instead of *fructibus*) or *sitim*. But these words are not strange at all, they are only the remnants of Old Latin forms. When I began writing Latin poems one day I asked myself: 'Would it be possible to write a poem in Old Latin?'. The answer is *Niuis Mundus*. Here I tried to use the most important phonetic and morphologic features of Old Latin, but I kept the syntax simple, so that the text is not too 'alien'. Besides I wrote two versions of my poem (one in Old Latin and one in Classical Latin), in order to make comprehension easier. As far as the theme of my poem is concerned, I had the first idea of *Niuis Mondos* while reading Goethe's *Erlkönig*. Here, however, the ending is happier.

Niuis Mundus (Classical Latin)

it homo candidas per siluas,
caelum est niuis, terra glaciei.
arboribus sunt foliae nullae.
uiator fessus est, sed iter etiamdum longum.
uentus susurrat ei uerba dulcia,
pollicitur niueum lectum, quietem.
at homo scit hoc dolum esse.

nox appropinquat celer,
tenebrae iam uincunt lucem,
aer fit frigidus quasi sol non esset.
uiator sistit aspicitque lucum circum se.
audit uoces subtiles folium herbarumque,
lucus totus eum inuitat ad requiescendum.
homo cunctatur, sed pedes eius graues sunt.

astra in caelo micant, etsi uiator ea non uidet,
quia oculi illius iam clauduntur.
dormiturus est, sed repente uenit auis super se.
parua luscinia eum monet suauisono cantu.
uiator ob stuporem rursum uigil auem sequitur,
siluam sub luna stellisque lucentem transit,
ad oppidum peruenit. at luscinia interea euanescuit.

Niuis Mundos (Old Latin)

eid homo candidans per siluans,
caelom est niuis, tera glacieis,
arbosebus sont foliai nulai.
uiator fesos est, set iter etiamdom longom.
uentos susurat ei uerba dulcia,
policitor niueom lectom, quietem,
at homo scit hoce dolom esse.

29

nox apropinquat celer,
tenebrai iam uincont lucem,
aer fit fricidos, quasi sol non essed,
uiator sisteid aspeceidque loucom circom sed.
audit uoceis subtilis foliom herbasomque,
loucos totos im inuitat ad requiescendom.
homo qunctator, set pedeis eius grauis sont.

astra in caelod micant, etsi uiator ea non uidet,
quia oquloi illius iam clauduntor.
dormituros est, set repente ueneid auis super sed.
parua luscinia im monet suauisonod cantud.
uiator ob stuposem rursu uigil auim sequitor,
siluam sub lunad stelaisque loucentem transeit,
ad opidom perueneit. at luscinia interea euanesqued.

Metre: Free verses

Translation: *Snow World.*

> A man goes through white woods,
> the sky is made of snow, the earth of ice.
> On the trees there are no leaves.
> The traveller is tired, but the way is still long.
> The wind whispers sweet words,
> promises a snowy bed, quiet.
> But the man knows this is deceit.
>
> Night comes near swiftly,
> darkness overcomes light,
> the air becomes cold, as if the sun didn't exist.
> The traveller stops and looks at the place around him.
> He hears the subtle voices of leaves and herbs,
> all wood is praying him to take rest.
> The man hesitates, but his feet are heavy.
>
> The stars shine in the sky, though the traveller does not see them,
> because his eyes are already closing.
> He is almost sleeping, but suddenly a bird comes overhead.
> A small nightingale warns him with a charming song.
> The traveller, again awake by astonishment, follows the bird,
> goes through the forest, glittering under the moon and the stars, comes
> finally to a town. Meanwhile the nightingale has disappeared.

*   *   *

Romae Occasus

Marco writes: I had the first idea of *Romae Occasus* when studying the Fall of the Western Roman Empire. We read in almost all books that 476 indicates the beginning of the Middle Ages, but very few people understood it then. As Odoacer compelled the young Romulus Augustulus to abdicate, the situation of Italy was already helpless. On the other hand, the sack of Rome of 410 was a real blow for the Latin prestige: the city had not been conquered since Brennus (390 B.C.). The news (*Roma capta!*) created great sorrow all over the Empire and it was one of the main reason why Augustine wrote his *De Civitate Dei*. In this poem I try to imagine the feelings of the Romans who saw their world fading before their eyes.

stabat Roma peritura
propter hostes ruitura
barbarorum circumdata
ira Deis non seruata.

spectat Gothos inter fora,
Consul fugit sine mora.
templa Iouis sunt uastata.
domus Sullae populata.

non sunt duces exhortantes,
non cohortes oppugnantes.
corda procul nunc honore,
metus certat cum pudore.

ubi Cato, ubi Titus?
ubi Romanus abitus?
iam sepulchri uetustorum
gemunt omnes senatorum.

Alarice, quid fecisti?
mundi caput occidisti.
est nunc templum ciuitatum
prope gothis iam necatum.

complet fletus matronarum
auras atque puellarum.
parcitur non senectute,
nemo domo sua tute.

fax Latina iam non splendet.
quis nunc orbis lumen prendet?

31

improuise nox appetit.
umbra nigra cuncta cepit

Noua Roma Constantini,
Liui domus, Augustini,
Imperatrix populorum,
serua flammam Romanorum!

Metre: Rhythmic Trochaic

Translation: *Rome's Sunset*

Rome laid, doomed,
Falling because of her enemies,
Surrounded by the barbarians' wrath,
Protected no more by her gods.

She sees the Goths in the *fora*,
The consul runs away without delay,
The temples of Jupiter are destroyed,
Sulla's house plundered.

There are no generals who exhort,
No troops who fight,
The hearts are now without honour,
Fear struggles with blame.

Where is Cato? Where is Titus?
Where has the Roman gone off?
All ancient senators'
Sepulchres already groan.

Alaric, what have you done?
You've slayed the world's capital.
The temple of cities has been
Almost killed by the Goths.

The weeping of matrons and girls
Fills up the air.
The old age is not spared,
One is no more secure at home.

The Latin torch has ceased to shine,
Who will now take in his hand the world's light?
The night falls unexpectedly,
A dark shadow has taken hold of everything.

New Rome of Constantine,
Livy's and Augustine's house,
Nations' empress,
Preserve the Romans' torch!

*   *   *

32

Amalasuintha Lux Hesperiae

Marco writes: Amalasuntha was the daughter of Theoderic, king of the Ostrogoths, and of Audofleda, a Frankish princess. She grew up in Ravenna together with Cassiodorus and Boethius. Around 515 she married Eutharicus, a Goth from Spain. He should have inherited the kingdom, but he died suddenly, leaving his wife alone with a child, Athalaric. In 526 Theoderic passed away and Amalasuntha became regent of Italy. She was a learned woman and a great queen, perhaps the best Italy has ever had. But the Goths didn't like her: she was too 'Roman' and they claimed that Athalaric should be brought up according to the Gothic traditions. The queen had to agree, but it was a bad choice: the young king died in 534 of drunkness. At this point Amalasuntha was in a difficult situation: a woman could not reign alone. So she associated to the throne her cousin Theodahad. He promised to leave her all power, but then he exiled and killed her in 535.

olim regina Gothorum,
olim decus Amalorum,
olim spes Urbis Romanae,
nomen triste nunc inane
in astris abscondita.

magno rege Gotho patre,
est nata Francaque matre.
adoleuit cum romanis,
christianis et mundanis
libris semper dedita.

liberos rex non habebat,
sic regni heres fiebat
qui ducebat hanc uxorem.
nupta patitur dolorem
morte uix credita.

post obitum Eutharici
mater est Athalarici
facta mox regina Gothum.
Mulier habet regnum totum,
res numquam tradita.

Amalasuintha sola
sed non est magnaque mola
est regni Cassiodoro
quoque sumpta cum decoro,
nulla fama perdita.

Gothi tandem non omnino
reginam corde Latino
ferunt et antiquo more
uolunt regem cum clamore
cresci, fide abdita.

Athalaricus uitiis
fauet Gothis cum sociis.
Baccho nimis eneruatus
munus obit insectatus,
uita dis impedita.

corde matris sic occiso
regina bello prouiso
ad Theodahdo seruandum
nubit regnum, at nefandum
nescit uirum prodita.

malus proditor uxoris,
uir praui saeuique moris
reginam rapit et necat.
Sic is spei fila secat
auri ui recondita.

Amalasuinthae finis
haec uitae, sed non Latinis
lucis reginae Gothorum,
quae nunc splendet Romanorum
terris iam expedita.

Metre: Rhythmic

Translation: *Amalasuntha, The Light of Hesperia*

Once queen of the Goths,
once glory of the Amals,
once hope of the city of Rome,
now sad and empty name,
she is hidden among the stars.

Her father was a powerful Gothic king,
she was born from a Frankish woman.
She became adult among the Romans,
reading very often Christian
and pagan books.

The king did not have sons,
so kingdom's heir would become
the man who'd marry her.
She wed, but suffered a great pain,
because of an unpredictable death.

After Eutharic passed away
the mother of Athalaric
was queen of the Goths.
A woman had a whole kingdom,
no one had ever seen such an event.

But Amalasuntha was not
alone and the heavy millstone
of the reign was also sustained
honourably by Cassiodorus,
with no loss of fame.

The Goths, however, didn't love
utterly a queen with a Latin heart
and they claimed loudly that the king
should be brought up according to the barbarian
traditions, having lost the trust in their queen.

Athalaric behaved viciously
with his Gothic friends.
Weakened by Bacchus,
he died having despised his duty,
his life was forbidden by the gods.

The mother's heart was almost transfixed,
but she saw in advance the impending war,
so she married Teodahad
in order to save the kingdom,
but she, betrayed, did not know the man.

The evil traitor of his wife,
a man perverse and cruel,
kidnapped and slaughtered the queen.
Thus he cut the hope's threads
because of the hidden force of gold.

This is the end of Amalasuntha's
life, but not, for the Latins,
of the Gothic queen's light,
which now shines free
above the Roman country.

*   *   *

Theodahatus Tyrannus

Marco writes: Theodahad had two hobbies: philosophy and the neighbour's land.
When he lived in Tuscany he used to rob the other landowners of their estates.
In 535 he decided to became a kingdom-robber, but he soon understood that
ruling Italy was not a pleasant job. So he tried to sell the country to the emperor

Justinian. The talks went on for a year, but the Goths suspected Theodahad, so in 536 they elected a new king, Witiges. Theodahad ran away at once towards Ravenna (he was probably going to sail to Byzantium), but a Gothic soldier cut his head before he could reach the city. As the reader will see, I am not very fond of Theodahad. And I'm not the only one: the *Cambridge Medieval History* (Volume II, p. 15) describes him as "impressionable, changeable, unsteady, unreliable, and, in addition, a coward".

fur Theodahadus
regni uero gradus
dolo conscendisti
et clam necauisti
reginam, tyranne!

Tusci latro agri,
rex mentis onagri,
philosophe uilis,
dux Gothis hostilis,
proditor, tyranne!

coronam foedasti,
fidem uiolasti,
regnum tradidisti,
pauide fugisti
ad hostes, tyranne!

at sors imminebat,
hora nam ruebat:
Gothus tibi cepit
caput, non decepit
fatum tunc, tyranne!

Metre: Rhythmic

Translation: *Theodahad the Tyrant*

Thief Theodahad,
the kingdom's stairs
thou climbed deceitfully
and thou killed in secret
the queen, tyrant!

Thief of the Tuscan land,
ass-minded king,
coward philosopher,
ruler enemy of the Goths,
traitor, tyrant!

36

Thou polluted the crown,
thou dishonoured the promises
thou surrendered the kingdom,
thou ran away trembling
to the enemies, tyrant!

But the lot overhung,
the hour was rushing away:
a Goth cut your
head, you didn't
deceive the fate, tyrant!

*   *   *

Senatus Romae Sexto Saeculo

Marco writes: In August 2014 I finished writing my Bachelor thesis about the Roman Senate in the VI Century. I printed and gave it to my thesis supervisor, who told me to write a summary of my work (109 pages) in no more than three pages: every candidate has only ten minutes to summarize his/her work! I had to do many heart-breaking cuts, but then I asked myself: why not writing a rhythmical summary in Latin? I wondered a bit whether to recite it during the academic defense, but then I preferred not to...

Roma lapsa stat senatus,
iter Urbis comitatus;
reges, consules, Augustos
fama dilexit onustos,
ampla, lata Curia.

barbari cum re potiti
senatores sunt muniti,
nam ut regnum ministrarent,
ne Romani rebellarent,
opus erat Curia.

Gothi sic honorant patres,
quasi quidem essent fratres;
Roma nondum occidente,
Hamalo rem tum regente,
magis splendet Curia.

at Boethio necato
Symmachoque mox delato,
umbra nigra cuncta cepit.
senatorum uox non strepit,
silescente Curia.

cum procella propinquaret,
Urbem ut et se seruaret,

37

Graecis omnes pandit portas
sperans pugnas tunc exortas
ire procul Curia.

bellum saeuit sed uiginti,
annos atque Gothi uinti
plures patres occiderunt.
pauci uix superfuerunt,
uanescente Curia.

Langobardis mox ingressis,
Romae ciuibus obsessis,
Dei Consul est creatus.
obmutescit nunc senatus,
psallitur in Curia.

Metre: Rhythmic

Translation: *The Roman Senate in the VI Century*

Once Rome fell, the Senate stood,
attending the City's journey;
the ample, wide Curia
chose kings, consuls, emperors,
all laden with glory.

When barbarians went to power,
senators were secure,
in order to administer the kingdom,
to avoid rebellions by the Romans,
the Senate was needed.

Thus goths treated senators with respect,
as if they were brothers;
Rome has not yet set down,
a Hamal was governing Italy
and Curia shined more than before.

But Boethius was killed,
Symmachus was accused
and a black shadow covered everything.
The voice of senators did not even murmur,
Curia was becoming silent.

When the storm drew near,
to save the City and themselves,
they opened all gates to the Greeks,
hoping that the war then arisen
would be fought far away

But the conflict raged for twenty
years and the defeated goths
killed lots of senators.
Few hardly survived,

Curia was vanishing.

Soon the Langobards arrived,
the citizens of Rome were besieged
and a consul of God was created.
Now the Senate became mute,
hymns were sung in the Curia.

*   *   *

Kemar Cummings

Kemar Cummings lives in Jamaica, where he earned a B.A. in Literatures in English with First Class Honours. He has published poetry in publications such as *Bookends, sx salon* and *Tongues of the Ocean*.

Amor Cordis

Kemar writes: This poem was written a few years ago while I was trying to teach myself Latin. I love classical poetry and when I saw that other people are still writing Latin verse I thought I might try to write one myself.

> *tu, domina mea, flammas passionis incendet. Amor,*
> *arco magno, certe cor celeri sagitta iacet.*
> *autem amoris venti in pectore meo flagrant*
> *pro hac, meum cor in ardore movet*

Metre: Free verse

Translation: *A Love of the Heart.*

> You, my lady, ignites the flames of love. Love,
> With a great bow, is sure to strike my heart with its arrow.
> As the winds of love flame up in my breast
> For her, my heart moves in love.

*   *   *

Chris de Lisle, Hanna Mason, Sam Howell

Chris de Lisle, Hanna Mason and Sam Howell were MA
students in Classics at Victoria University of Wellington in New
Zealand and members of the Latin Poetry Composition Group
there.

Alliterative Achilles

Chris writes: The Latin poetry composition group at Victoria University of
Wellington (New Zealand) was made up of students from second year to
postgraduate level, who met every Wednesday to write verse. Sometimes we
produced something with which we were (not so) quietly chuffed. The current
piece, inspired by the story of Niobe at *Iliad* 26.603 and fragments of Ennius, is
one example:

> *Pelides Priamo ploranti poplite prono:*
> *'Annuto. nemo nescit Niobae necopina*
> *dona deorsum dis. Deli deus atque Diana,*
> *Tantalides transfixerunt telo terebrante.*
> *in luteum lapidem lacrimosa illiberis illa*
> *mutata est. maeres modo motus imagine mortis*
> *sed satis est solaminis in saxo Sipyleo?'*

Metre: Alliterative Hexameters

Translation:

> Peliad Achilles to Priam, prone, begging on his knees:
> 'I assent. None know not Niobe's unexpected
> donations down to the gods. Delos' deity and Diana,
> thrust through the Tantalides, her children, with tearing arrows.
> Childless, crying, she was converted into a crusty crag.
> Now you mourn, moved by the image of mortality,
> but is there solace enough in Sipylean stone?'

*   *   *

Kyle Gervais

Kyle Gervais is an assistant professor of Classics at the University of Western Ontario. He studies the greatest works of Western literature (Latin epic, of course), but is the child of an ironic generation. So in his spare time, he writes poems about the little lives of rabbits and squirrels.

Garett Schoffro is an undergraduate student in Classics and in the School for Advanced Studies in the Arts and Humanities at the University of Western Ontario. He plays tennis, hockey, and the guitar. He also excels at Latin, and sketches rabbits with speed and aplomb.

Sciurus Interfectus

Kyle writes: Once on a Thanksgiving I had the displeasure of seeing one of London, Ontario's happy black squirrels run over by an SUV. Overwhelmed by the injustice of the universe, I fought back with an elegy and an invective. I borrow from Horace, Catullus, and Virgil, all of whom knew better than I how to deal with these disasters of life.

> *parue, miser, subito interfecte, o pulle sciure,*
> *summa breuis uitae spes hiemis secuit.*
> *monstrum ingens praeceps celeres frustra obruit artus,*
> *uoluens per gelidam corpus inane uiam.*
> *irrita uita fuit, mors illacrimabilis (esto):*
> *fama perennis erit, pulle sciure, tua.*
>
> *inflammabo ego te atque uerberabo,*
> *monstrum ingens, nocuum nigro sciuro!*
> *conculcabo (mihi illa sit potestas)*
> *rectorem quoque conscium atque caecum!*
> *tabes corpora uestra digna edet mox;*
> *fama et gloria erit perennis illi.*

Metre: Elegiac couplets and hendecasyllables

Translation:

> Poor little suddenly slaughtered black squirrel,
> your brief lifespan has cut off your hopes for the winter.
> A huge, hurtling monster has crushed your vainly skittering limbs,
> rolling your dead body down the cold road.
> Your life was fruitless, your death unmourned (so be it):
> the story of you, little black squirrel, will endure.

I'll scorch you and scourge you,
huge monster who hurt the black squirrel!
And I'll stomp (if only I could)
on your driver, so guilty and blind!
Worthy rot will eat your two bodies soon enough;
his glorious story will endure.

*   *   *

Reading Ovid

Kyle writes: Ovid, like all poets, leaves a lot unwritten. Here are a few short poems that fill in (what I see as) gaps in scenes from *Metamorphoses* 8-10.

Met. 8.183-259

Ovid relates, in reverse chronological order, the accidental death of Daedalus' son Icarus and Daedalus' earlier murder of his nephew Perdix (8.250f. *Daedalus inuidit sacraque ex arce Mineruae / praecipitem misit, lapsum mentitus*). Somehow, the reordering of the stories made me wonder what *really* happened to Icarus (after all, Daedalus, a proven child-killer, was the only witness). In any case, the *pater infelix* (8.231) seems to have been unusually unlucky when it came to boys in his care!

> *Daedalus infelix dum spectat, natus in undas*
> *Icarias cecidit, ceciditque ex arce Mineruae*
> *altera dum spectas, infelix Daedale, proles.*

Translation:

> While unlucky Daedalus looked on, his son fell
> into the Icarian waves, and from the citadel of Minerva
> another son fell, unlucky Daedalus, while you looked on.

Met. 8.260-444

Meleager son of Oeneus gives the spoils of the Calydonian Boar to Atalanta (here named after the Arcadian town of Tegea). Meleager kills his two uncles, sons of Thestius, after they take the spoils from her. The issue of women speaking and not speaking is important in Ovidian studies, and it struck me that throughout the entire episode of the hunt and its aftermath, while male heroes bluster and threaten and brag, the all-important Atalanta never says a word.

> *Thestiadae uiolant tacitae laudes Tegeaeae:*
> *hos necat Oenides dum Tegeaea tacet.*

Translation:

> The sons of Thestius insult the accomplishments of the silent Tegean:
> the son of Oeneus kills them, while the Tegean stays silent.

Met. 9.159-272

As he dies in slow agony, Hercules delivers an improbably long speech to complain of his unending persecution by Juno. The 'famous son of Jupiter' (9.229 *Iouis inclita proles*) sums up this divine injustice with a hyperbolically odd bit of atheism: *et sunt, qui credere possint / esse deos?* (9.203-4) Then he is apotheosized. But poor Deianira, whose only crime is not wanting Hercules to leave her for another woman, is left behind anyway by her newly divine husband—and by Ovid, who doesn't mention her at all during or after Hercules' death.

> *'suntne', satus Ioue quaesiuit, 'qui credere possint*
> *esse deos?' deus est. est Deianira relicta.*

Translation:

> 'Is there anyone', asked the son of Jupiter, 'who could believe
> that the gods exist?' Now *he* is a god, but Deianira is abandoned.

Met. 10.106-219

Metamorphoses 10 is partly a study of all-conquering love, and so when Orpheus, the central figure of the book, tries to recover from his love for his dead wife, he fails: *uicit Amor* (10.26). But at the same time, over and over in the book, objects of love fall victim to accidental death—Adonis, Eurydice, Cyparissus' stag, and Hyacinthus (the two young boys, loves of Apollo the god of foresight, get the epithet *imprudens*, which inspired my poem). Love may conquer all like Virgil says but—for Venus, Orpheus, Cyparissus, and Apollo in their grief—I doubt it seemed that way at the time.

> *perdidit imprudens ceruum Cyparissus amatum;*
> *imprudens periit Hyacinthus Apolline amatus:*
> *omnia qui domuit domat imprudentia amorem.*

Translation:

> Cyparissus accidentally killed the stag that he loved;
> Hyacinth, loved by Apollo, died accidentally:
> accidents conquer love, which conquers all.

*   *   *

Certamen Choronzonis et Morpheos

Kyle writes: In issue 4 of Neil Gaiman's *The Sandman* our hero Morpheus, The King of Dreams, travels to Hell to retrieve his stolen helm, which he finds in the possession of the demon Choronzon (High Duke of the Eighth Circle, Captain of the Horde of Lord Beelzebub). Dream wins back his property in a remarkable contest. The idiomatic metre for amoebean verse like this is probably dactylic hexameter (cf. Virgil, *Eclogues* 3), but I had galliambic metre on the brain (cf. Catullus 63) when I tackled this. And really, Hell seems like an appropriate place for a duel in wild galliambics, whose basic Catullan form (˘ ˘ ¯ ˘ ˘ ¯ ˘ ˘ | ¯ ˘ ˘ ¯ ˘ ˘ ¯) can shift dramatically via resolution, contraction, and anaclasis (¯ ˘ ˘ ¯ ˘ ˘ | ¯ ¯ ¯ ˘ ˘ ¯ ; ˘ ˘ ¯ ˘ ˘ ¯ ˘ ˘ | ¯ ¯ ¯ ˘ ˘ ¯ ; ˘ ˘ ¯ ˘ ˘ ¯ ˘ ˘ | ¯ ¯ ¯ ˘ ˘ ¯ ; etc.). My free adaptation is followed by Gaiman's original.

> *Acherontis in profundo certant dei duo,*
> *daemon Stygis Choronzon Morpheusque callidus:*

[C] *'ego sum malus lupus qui praedam sequitur atrox.'*

[M] *'feriam ut lupum furentem, uenans ego eques ero.'*

[C] *'ego sum tabanus asper: rabido ruis ab equo.'*

[M] *'ego asilum itaque momordi, pede crebro eum tenens.'*

[C] *'ego araneam comedi: tibi toxica bibita.'*

[M] *'bos sum, pedes graues sunt, serpentem et obterunt.'*

[C] *'letale uirus, anthrax, animas ego aboleo.'*

[M] *'ego tellus, chaos interlabor, foueo animas.'*

[C] *'noua sum, ruina cunctis, orbi crematio.'*

[M] *'ego cuncta comprehendo, cunctas teneo animas:*
> *cuncta uniuersitas sum.'*

[C]   *'Mors Iudiciaque ego,*
> *ego in exitu omnium nox, ego diuum, ego orbium,*
> *ego sum uniuersitatis finis. quid itaque tu*
> *eris?' incola Erebi atrocis sic sibilat.*

[M]   *'ego spes.'*

Metre: Galliambic

English original:

[C]   'I am a dire wolf, prey-stalking, lethal power.'
[M]   'I am a hunter, horse-mounted, wolf-stabbing.'
[C]   'I am a horsefly, horse-stinging, hunter-throwing.'
[M]   'I am a spider, fly-consuming, eight legged.'
[C]   'I am a snake, spider-devouring, poison-toothed.'
[M]   'I am an ox, snake-crushing, heavy footed.'
[C]   'I am anthrax, butcher bacterium, warm-life destroying.'
[M]   'I am a world, space-floating, life nurturing.'
[C]   'I am a nova, all-exploding, planet-cremating'.
[M]   'I am the Universe—all things encompassing, all life embracing.'
[C]   'I am anti-life, the Beast of Judgment. I am the dark at the end of everything. The end of universes, gods, worlds . . . of everything. Sss. And what will you be then, Dreamlord?'
[M]   'I am hope.'

*   *   *

Carmina Leporina

Kyle writes: In 2014 a student in my Introductory Latin class named Garett Schoffro not only thoroughly mastered any Latin I taught, but sketched the ongoing misadventures of a rabbit on the back of each week's quiz paper. These seemed as good a subject as any for poetry, so I responded with a short poem each week. The sketches were each done in about 5 minutes, the poems in 15-60 minutes—*subito calore et quadam festinandi uoluptate*, as Statius would say (*Silvae* 1 *praef.*)

(1) Hello! (first quiz)

> *sic laudo lepidum leporem saluere iubentem.*

(2) Argh!

> *en piraticus apparuit lepus, atque galerum*
> *in capite atque gerens tegumentum in lumine laeuo.*
> *ille ferox fremit "Argh!" (uox illa fremenda Latine est).*

(3) Harey Potter

> *"Expelliarmus!" dicere uisus est*
> *cuniculus qui uitra ocularia*
> *nec non cicatricem ferebat*
> *fulminis exitialis instar.*

(4) Prima Porta Rabbit (on the back of a take-home quiz)

> *o labor egregius! res optima! facta uenusta!*
> *en leporem cerno, quem splendidiore peregit*
> *quam solitus calamo pictoribus ille Garettus*
> *cunctis (qui calamo lepores depingere sueti)*
> *clarior! ante oculos leporina Augustus aenus*
> *stat uersus forma: leporis coma nobilis aures*

germinat, a leporis laeua toga mascula pendet,
lorica lepus est tectus, leporaria dextra
tollitur. ad crus non Amor (ecce!) lepusculus astat.

(5) Shark

carcharus (heu!) leporem submersum territat ingens.

(6) Easter

ego nidum uideo ouis uiduum cum lepore illo;
leporem insidere nido uideo (o res memoranda!) et
    lepidum ouum radiare.

(7) Trampoline

salitque securus,
Cuniculus salit

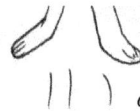

assurgens.
sursus
cadens   *atque*
deorsus

cunicule (o caue, caue!) infideles sunt
inutilesque,
     inepte,
          trampolini
               nunc!

They don't make trampolines like they used to

FIN

48

(8) *Vale!* (final exam)

> *ille lepus quondam qui me saluere iubebat*
> *nunc lacrimas manans triste ualere iubet.*
> *o lepidissime tu leporum, ualeas aueasque;*
> *tu quoque, discipulorum optime, aue atque uale!*

Valē, Dr. Gervais

(9) Epilogue (summertime)

> *absunt discipuli; tacuere academica tecta;*
> *non mihi sunt lepores; carmina nostra silent.*

Metres: Hexameters (poems 1, 2, 4, 5), Alcaic stanza (3), scazons (6), ionics *a minore* (7), elegiac couplets (8, 9)

Materials: Black ink and highlighter (sketch 7) on the back of quiz papers

Translation:

(1)

This is how I praise the charming rabbit that's saying hello.

(2)

Look! A pirate-rabbit has shown up, wearing a hat
on his head and a patch on his left eye.
He fiercely growls "Argh!" (that sound should be growled in Latin).

(3)

"*Expelliarmus!*", the rabbit seemed to say
who was wearing eye glasses
and of course a scar
in the shape of a deadly lightning bolt.

(4)

O wonderful work! Thing of excellence! Charming creation!
Look—I see a rabbit worked out with a pen more distinguished
than usual by the famous Garett, who is more illustrious
than all the artists (the ones whose pens are in the habit of
drawing
rabbits). A bronze Augustus stands before my eyes,
but changed into the shape of a rabbit: his noble hair sprouts
rabbit ears; his manly toga hangs from a rabbit's left hand;
it's a rabbit that's covered by the breastplate, a rabbit's right
hand
raised up. At his feet stands no Cupid—look!—but a little bunny.

(5)

Oh sh*t! A giant shark is frightening the rabbit underwater.

(6)

I see a nest bereft of eggs along with that rabbit;
I see the rabbit sit on the nest (what a remarkable thing!) and
   a pretty egg shine.

(7)

The carefree rabbit jumps and jumps,
falling down and rising up.
Silly rabbit (o, beware, beware!)—trampolines are
unreliable and useless nowadays!

(8)

That rabbit which once said hello to me
   now sheds tears and sadly says goodbye.
You, oh most charming of rabbits, goodbye and farewell;
   you too, best of students, farewell and goodbye.

(9)

The students are gone; the buildings are quiet;
   I have no more rabbits; our songs now fall silent.

*   *   *

Patrick Paul Hogan

Patrick Paul Hogan is an independent Classical scholar in the United States who currently works as a proofreader and translator for Brill. He is especially proud of his contributions to the new *Brill Dictionary of Ancient Greek* (2015). A 2005 graduate of the PhD program in Classical Philology at the University of Michigan, he has taught at colleges and universities in Michigan and serves on the board of *Amphora*, the outreach publication of the American Philological Association. He is the midst of a multi-year project to memorize the *Eclogues* of Vergil at a verse or two per day, and he spends his evenings translating the poems of the *Epigrammata Graeca* OCT of Page into what he hopes is decent Latin. He contributes here two original compositions.

Mus Apud Me

Patrick writes: In the Fall of 2012 I took up writing Latin poetry, mostly because of my experience at the Inter Versiculos Conference at the University of Michigan in Ann Arbor in the summer of 2011, where David Money led many neophytes on their first steps into this arena, but also because of the new venues like *Vates* that have appeared of late. This poem is based on an incident in late 2012 at my mother's house – although I must admit that the affair ended rather fatally for the mouse. We are still waiting to see if his *amici* will come. I would like to thank Prof. Kristopher Fletcher for reviewing drafts of the poem and for his perceptive and kind comments.

plus cibi et melius libens parassem
sed O muscule te futurum apud me
nesciui. mea mensa pauperata est
et penaria cella plena solis
tenebris (bene scis) araneisque.
est opus mihi liberalitate
siue aduenerit inuocatus hospes
siue sit coquus aeger ebriusue
siue putrida sit caro uel absens.
praesens es meus hospes et saluto
te. nec Iuppiter hospitum deus sit
iratus feriatque me seuere
claro fulgure nec lupum ferocem
memet efficiat nefas ob atrum
ut est passus et impius Lycaon.
ipsum autem rapuisse frustulum te
aequum aduerto animum sed hoc remitto;

bene hoc est: fruere et tua rapina
et magna nimiaque comitate
mea, sed precor O gulose noli
amicis facere hanc palam tabernam.
nonne caseoli satis tibi est nunc?
an panis satis? estne sic? beate
cenandum est, sed agas mihi pusillas
gratias aliquasue liberali.
eccum! ianitor it meus celox ut
te deducat honore curioso;
feles officio suo uidetur
perfungi cupida esse. quam fidelis!
uale, bestia cara; si redibis,
amabo; modo nuntium antemittas.

Metre: Hendecasyllables

Translation:

I would have willingly prepared more food, but little mouse, I did not know that you would be at my house. Mine is a pauper's table and my pantry is full of only shadows and cobwebs, as you well know. I must be generous whether a   guest will show up uninvited, or the cook is sick or drunk, or the meat is rotten or missing. You are here as a guest and I welcome you. May Jupiter, the god of guests, not be angry and strike me down severely with a bright thunderbolt nor turn me into a wild wolf because of black sin, as impious Lycaon once suffered. Now I calmly notice that you have snatched a bit for yourself, but I let this go; it is all right: enjoy both your plunder and my great and perhaps overmuch friendliness, but I beg you, O glutton, do not reveal this tavern to your friends. Is there enough cheese for you now? Enough bread? Yes? Dine quite well, but do give small or at least some thanks for my generosity. Behold! My doorkeeper comes quickly so that she might lead you out carefully in honor; my cat seems to be eager to enjoy her duty. How faithful! Goodbye, dear beast; if you return, I will be happy; just send a messenger ahead.

*   *   *

Ad Alexandrum

Patrick writes: This poem is addressed to a Greek student of mine who entered graduate school in Classics in the fall of 2013. In it I wish him well in his future studies and reflect on the constant campaigns of scholarship. I would like to thank Prof. Kristopher Fletcher for reviewing drafts of the poem and for his insightful comments.

Alexander auare priscioris
doctrinae (uitium quod optimum esse
declaro et mihi iamdiu aestimatum),

eras discipulus laboriosus:
docto macte animo! sed hinc eundum est
ut discas aliunde pleniusque.
nec curae tibi cursus est honorum
neque est scaena decora nec coronae
quas Mars militibus dedit salutans.
nil noui, iuuenis, nihil pudoris!
audi ueridicum: libens senesco
magister modo tot libris legendis
saepe discipulis tot edocendis
sed semper quasi lege perseuera
omnis est mea uota litteris mens.
nam me terribilis tenet cupido
illarum ex puero meum ad sepulchrum.
tali amore uideris illaqueri
ut in reticulo lepus latenti.
hoc times? agedum timere noli!
nam dulcissima nostra seruitudo
qualem olim facile Hercules ferebat
cum texebat in Omphales diaeta.
neque umquam timeas struem librorum:
ille cum Macedo ducis Philippi
stabat filius ipse in Asianis
ripis, eminuere regna magna
quae solus poterat deus tenere
Bacchus imperio suo patrisque,
regna non numeranda mente fessa.
at fuit cupidus laboris omnis
ut illustris in aeua gloria esset.
sic par nisus idemque nomen insunt:
tunc ad ultima uincere orbis illi,
nunc transis mare tu libens librorum.
et Musae tibi opem ferant canorae
atque Mnemosyne det uber album
ut istam satiet sitim perennem.
si placet tibi, nuntios remitte
inter proelia magna, miles audax,
cum rare ueniant breues quietes.
at noli tamen huc remittere illos:
scito me abfore. num putas magistrum
nos Aristotelem domi restare?
uix! stipendia longa demerebo
neque umquam rediturus ipse uictor.

53

nam nos inuenient benigna Fata
discentem sine termino et quiete.

Metre: Hendecasyllables

Translation:

Alexander, hungry for the ancient learning (a vice which I declare to be
the best and valued by me for a long time now), you were a hard-working
student: well done for your learned mind! But now you must go away to
learn from another teacher and more fully. The pursuit of offices is of no
concern for you nor the glorious stage nor the crowns that saluting Mars
has given to soldiers. This is nothing new, young man, nothing shameful!
Listen to one who speaks the truth: gladly do I grow old as a teacher now
in the reading of so many books, often in the instructing of so many
students, but always as if by a very rigorous law my whole mind is
devoted to letters. For a terrible desire for them holds me from boyhood
to grave. With such a love you seem to be ensnared as a hare in a
hidden net. Do you fear this? Come now, don't be afraid! For our
servitude is most sweet like the one that Hercules once bore easily when
he was weaving in Omphale's apartment. Nor should you ever fear the
heap of books: when that Macedonian, the son of the general Philip,
stood on Asian shores himself, great kingdoms loomed before him, ones
that the god Bacchus alone was able to hold with his own power and that
of his father, kingdoms not to be numbered by a weary mind. But he was
desirous of every labor so that he might have illustrious glory forever. So
you and he have an equal striving and the same name: back then it was
his aim to conquer to the ends of the earth, now may you cross the sea of
books gladly. May the singing Muses bring you aid and Mnemosyne give
you her white breast so that she quench your perennial thirst. If it
pleases you, send back messengers amid the great battles, brave soldier,
whenever brief moments of rest rarely come. But yet do not send them
back here: know that I will be away. You don't think me to be the teacher
Aristotle staying at home, do you? Hardly! I will earn my pay for long
service and I will never return a victor. For the kindly Fates will find me
learning without end or respite.

*   *   *

James Houlihan

James Houlihan was born in Michigan, moved to Libya at nine months; then Weisbaden, Bethesda, the Mojave Desert, Dayton, and Santa Barbara. He currently lives and works in Houston. Ph.D. in Comparative Literature; M.A. and B.A. in Classics (University of California, Santa Barbara; all). Recent poems in *Metamorphoses*, *InTranslation*, *RiverSedge*, *moria*, *Monkeybicycle*. Previous publications: *Thirty-One Superior Poems of Our Time* (Inleaf Press, 2004) and *Driving Cabeza* (Inleaf Press, 2000). "Incorporating the Other; the Catalogue of Women in Odyssey 11" [*Diotima*]. Translation: (with F. Fagundes) Jorge de Sena, *The Art of Music* (University Editions, 1998).

Lesbia ad Catullum

James writes: The two poems in Sapphic stanzas imagine Lesbia/Clodia, *docta puella*, responding as a poet to Catullus, translating a Sappho poem and writing a *renuntio amoris*.

(1) Claudia translationem sapphicam ad Catullum mittens altera cum carmine

SAPPHO XVI

hos iuuant campi, mea lux, equorum,
nauis illos aut pedites micantes,
res mihi pulcherrima terrā opaca est
    quodquod amatum.

ueritatem perfacile est firmare:
quae eminebat in decore et fortuna,
coniugem diuum illa Helene reliquit
    enauigans, heu,

līberorum et progenitorum oblīta
rīsit inter Iliades abacta,
dum cito rorat species fulgore
    luminibus — quae

me monent Anactoriae meae nunc
perditae, nefas!, mihi, cui chorea

55

anteponenda est Lydiā formosa
conchyliata.

Metre: Sapphics

Translation (*Sappho* 16):

Some like fields of horses, my light,
others a ship or glittering infantries;
to me the most attractive thing on dark earth is
whatever is loved.

It's very easy to prove the truth: Helen
preeminent in grace and chance
abandoned a godlike husband
sailing—ah—away,

forgetting children and ancestors.
Seduced, she laughed among Trojan women,
beauty dripping by a quick gleam
from her eyes

which recall my Anacatoria
now lost to me—a crime. Her dancing
in shapliness I prefer to Lydia
dyed purple.

*   *   *

(2) Ad Catullum

diua, uoui, si restitutus ille
iam Catullus, clara mari creata,
si fuisset mi probus omnium pro
candida amore,

denique iambis trucibus relictis,
diua, uoui mox Volusi daturam
me et Vulcano carmina pessimorum
optima uatum.

non, poeta, ludes? ego et quoque aeque.
nunc scelus tuum retegam, dum imago
non redit nostrae pietatis umquam
immanioris.

cor meum thesaurus erat deusque,
et carina eram tua solque quondam.
errat intermundia quod dicebas,
candida ficta.

56

mene respectas simulans furorem?
ultima flos, Lesbia sum, uolabo,
mortua urbe conglaciato et orbe,
    spirituale.

Metre: Sapphics

Translation:

O sea-formed shining goddess, I swore
if that Catullus, restored to me now,
had been just with me
for our candor-bright love,

if finally the truculent iambic attacks stopped,
goddess, I swore I would burn
the best songs of Volusius and all
of the worst poets.

but if you won't play, poet—I, too, likewise, just the same.
I'll unroof your crime while a ghost-image
of our devotion never returns
more immense.

My heart was your treasury and god
and I was your ship and sun—once.
What you were saying wanders in the spaces between things,
candid-moral-bright fictions.

Do you respect me pretending madness?
the last flower, I am Lesbia, I will fly
when the City is dead and the universe frozen,
still breathing inspiration.

*   *   *

Elegia Cohensis

James writes: This is my Latin version of a Leonard Cohen poem, using a Horatian meter [e.g. 1.11]. The Cohen original follows, after which is a literal translation.

hunc ne quaesieris fluctibus in – quam gelidis! – altis
qui cantu crepitant suaviter in montibus bratteae.
sed caelestibus est non gradiendum ad loca frigida.
ne circumspicias reliquias, mollia corpora,
iratis in aquis. non lapides dant tibi sanguinem
ullo littore vasto. in calido tu sale tumido
amissum invenias qui cecidit per scopulos tardae

virescentis aquae. illum basiant agmina piscium
qui nidum peregrinum aedificant in corpore abs hieme
trito et aequora quod fugiat – heu mobile! – brandeum.

Metre: Fifth Asclepiad

English original:

> Do not look for him
> In brittle mountain streams:
> They are too cold for any god;
> And do not examine the angry rivers
> For shreds of his soft body
> Or turn the shore stones for his blood;
> But in the warm salt ocean
> He is descending through cliffs
> Of slow green water
> And the hovering coloured fish
> Kiss his snow-bruised body
> And build their secret nests
> In his fluttering winding-sheet. (© L. Cohen)

Literal translation:

> You should not search for him in streams – how icy – high
> that sweetly rattle with a song of gold foil in mountains.
> Gods cannot walk to cold places.
> You should not search for remains, a soft body,
> in angry waters. Stones don't give you his blood
> on any vast shore. You might in warm swelling saltwater
> find the lost one who fell past rocks of slow
> greening water. Formations of fish are kissing him
> and building a peregrine nest in his winter-bruised body
> and a funeral shroud – ah, wavering – to escape the sea.

*   *   *

Chris Kelk

Chris Kelk has an MA from St. Andrews, a Dip. Ed. from Oxford and an MA and PhD. from McMaster in Hamilton, Ontario. He spent two years teaching Latin in Freetown, Sierra Leone from 1967 to 1969 and has been a professional actor since 1973. He also won a medal at the Boston Marathon in 1975 with a time of 2:28:38!

Two Households

Chris writes: I was inspired to make this translation of the Prologue from *Romeo and Juliet* after acting in the play five times – each time as Friar Lawrence, though once I also played the Chorus.

> *in domibus magnis simili uirtute duabus*
> > *quo manifestatur pulchra Verona, dolor*
> *antiqui praesentia nunc fit facta cruoris*
> > *proeliaque ex odio sanguinolenta patent,*
> *sic cuiusque ex inguinibus fatalibus hostis,*
> > *mors homines geminos eligit atque capit.*
> *fortunisque malis, ea quae mactauerat omnes*
> > *(quam longe quis scit?) rixa sepulta suis,*
> *quo fatalis amor procederet atque periret*
> > *perrueretque domos ira paterna duas*
> *quae, nisi mors duplex, nulla est remouere potestas,*
> > *quisque actor uobis explicet arte bona.*
> *sic audite, precor, noster conabitur illa*
> > *qualiacumque errent praeripuisse labor.*

Metre: Elegiac couplets

Translation:

> Two households, both alike in dignity,
> In fair Verona, where we lay our scene,
> From ancient grudge break to new mutiny,
> Where civil blood makes civil hands unclean.
> From forth the fatal loins of these two foes
> A pair of star-cross'd lovers take their life;
> Whose misadventured piteous overthrows
> Do with their death bury their parents' strife.
> The fearful passage of their death-mark'd love,
> And the continuance of their parents' rage,
> Which, but their children's end, nought could remove,
> Is now the two hours' traffic of our stage;

The which if you with patient ears attend,
What here shall miss, our toil shall strive to mend.

(*Romeo and Juliet*, Prologue)

*   *   *

Cantus Canum

Chris writes: This is an old Rugby drinking song and is sung to the tune of *The Church's One Foundation*. As a professional actor, I frequently use it as a warm-up before a performance.

tempus erat: conuenerunt ad uina latrantes
  ut biberent hilares, curribus atque scaphis.
intrauere domum, figentes nomina libro,
  in pariete suum quisque pependit anum.
sedibus impletis, quidam horum sanguine mixtus,
  sordidus atque minor, nunc uocat 'ignis adest!'
terror corda canum quatit ut sic proximum anum illi
  captent currentes; maximus inde furor
possedit cunctos, aliena quod illa gerebant
  quae manifestabant liuida signa sibi.
ossum igitur canis ignorat, spectans alienum
  in dorso, dicens leniter: 'isne meus?'

Metre: Elegiacs

Translation: *The Dog Song*

The dogs they had a party, they came from near and far,
And some dogs came by aeroplane and some dogs came by car;
They came into the court-room and signed the visitors' book,
Then each dog took his arsehole and hung it on a hook.

Now all the dogs were seated, each mother's son and sire,
When a dirty little mongrel got up and shouted, 'Fire!'
The dogs were in a panic, they had no time to look –
Each took the nearest arsehole from off the nearest hook.

The dogs were very angry because it was so sore
To wear another's arsehole they'd never worn before.
And that it is the reason why a dog will leave his bone
To sniff another's arsehole in the hope that it's his own.

*   *   *

A View of Old Oxford

Chris writes: The poet John Barry and I were at grammar school together in Bradford and have remained friends. He is in the habit of sending me his poetry and I have quite a collection now. *A View of Old Oxford*, is, I think, his funniest.

optima, care nepos, noua mittis. gratulor atque
*   magna dedisse tibi Flumina Bina Boum*
praemia sum felix. essent quae facta requires,
*   dignane sint fama. sic tibi, Marce, loquor:*
o! prius Hellespontem atrum (sum frigoris osor!)
*   horrificumque natem quam reuidere locos*
illos constituam. cur? blanditiae mulieris
*   perpaucis aderant. Flumina Bina Boum*
expertes Veneris nos accepere, dolores
*   ut manifestarent – una puella uiris*
tris tribus. excepit speratam singulus unus
*   laurum, nil octo, languidolenta sibi*
murmura mussantes. hic docta est classica lingua
*   cuius nos unum novimus inde modum –*
optatum. gladius, duo qui prope crura residet,
*   illa sibi mandate quae sibi mandat Amor.*
in studiis nostris labuntur scripta Platonis,
*   candit, ut inficita praecipitetque calor*
antiplatonius o! mentes, non corpora, nostrae
*   inde colebantur. forsitan illa dies*
adueniet tandem cum, Flumina Bina putabant,
*   illi trans studiis sollicitata ferant*
ingenia, arte tamen nos auertere pudenda
*   multimodis somnis uisa. dedere nihil*
nostris scripta Latina boni scrotisue perustis
*   testiculiue nihil. 'somata nousi' (uides?)*
sunt immixta: magis gladiis quo corpora laesa
*   sunt, o! sicut eo non potis aëra sunt*
mentibus alta peti. quocumque puella per aulas
*   errabat, quidam 'femina bella prope!'*
omnibus inquit et insani tumidique studentes
*   illlam spectabant. et uagibundus, uti*
in uatis Stygiis umbris uir quisque petebat
*   quae loca quaeque silent, anxius esse procul.*
nil insanius est quam hoc fata sagacibus esse
*   decreuisse uiris; multa minora simul*

oppida quo discebatur sapientia magnos
  pulchrarum numeros cuique dedere uiro.
sed riuis latis similes flauis in harenis
  pectora tangenda et uagina lubrica errant
Fluminibus Binis, quas dilexere stuprosi
  quique libros spectant, ah! releuantque manu
se in Collis Viridis ludo seducere discit
  quisque puer pueras. euge! geresque bene.
forsitan agnosces dominas se iungere genti
  humanae: uerum hoc dicitur esse mihi.
tempora sed permutantur: tandem monachia
  nondum sunt illic (uae mihi!). uictor eris
in ludis Veneris, lacrimis placates egebis
  uanis. esto aliis uana fuisse memor.

Metre: Elegiacs

Translation: *A View of Old Oxford* by John Barry

John Barry read Classics Mods and English at The Queen's College, Oxford from
1962 to 1966. He is a retired schoolteacher and lives in Leeds, UK.

Dear Billy, thank you for your letter.
Fantastic news – I've not heard better
  For years and years.
What an achievement – to have won
An Oxford scholarship! Well done,
  Young genius. Cheers.

So now you write: "Dear Uncle John,
When you were up, what things went on,
  And what befell you?
Does it deserve its reputation?
And what's the social situation?"
  Well, lad, I'll tell you.

The truth, mind, not a lot of flannel.
And here it is. I'd swim the channel
  In March, both ways,
(I, that can hardly swim five feet
or bear cold) rather than repeat
  my Oxford days.

Surprised? I know the public thinks
Of student frolics and high jinks,
  Larks and excitement.
Why did I not find Oxford glamorous?
So little chance of being amorous –
  That's my indictment.

Our schools had all been single-sexed
And up to Oxford we came next,

62

To Queen's or Jesus.
What woeful tidings faced us then?
One female student per nine men!
    It didn't please us.

Write that in characters of flame:
NINE LUSTING FELLOWS FOR ONE DAME.
    For every winner
eight losers moped about and pined
each like a hungry dog that whined
    wanting its dinner.

We learnt the Latin tongue and Greek
And we could write them (though not speak)
    Like any native.
Gender and tense we understood,
Person and number, but one mood –
    Just the optative.

In such a case you don't need Freud
To tell how harmony's destroyed,
    What ills accrue.
However we ignore his cries,
The little gent between the thighs
    Demands his due.

So, grappling with Platonic prose,
Most unplatonic feelings rose
    To cause distraction.
Engaged with Ciceronian speeches
A stirring deep inside the breeches
    Demanded action –

But act on whom? No girls in sight.
They trained our nous with all their might
    Ignoring soma.
In colleges designed to bar us
From all that Helen did with Paris
    We read our Homer.

Perhaps they hoped that sublimation
Would foster mental exploration   -
    And there'd be sown
A love of Greek and Roman splendour.
But dreams of feminine pudenda
    Against our own

Expelled such visions from the head.
All that Hellenic stuff we read
    In verse or prose
Did not contribute one iota
To soothing our tormented scrota.
    Which only shows

Body and mind are linked together.
The mind has a restricted tether
    If somewhat lower
You feel a pain like prussic acid.
But, if that fellow's limp and placid,

63

The mind can soar.

As we sat quiet, seeking knowledge,
Sometimes a girl would pass the college.
    "A lass, a lass!"
someone would hollo to all present,
and mad and sad, hungry, tumescent,
    we'd watch her pass.

Or we would mope about the town
Like, when Odysseus journeyed down,
    The ghosts round Hades.
We had no focus for our lusts.
Our ancient halls were lined with busts,
    But none were ladies'.

And this – that's what's completely zany –
Was the result of being brainy.
    HAPPY THE STUPID!
While there was no-one to give US Sex
The Oxbridge failures down at SUSsex
    Made hay with Cupid.

They could enjoy their university,
No constant state of woman scarcity
    To get them down.
A desert drier than Arabia
For kissing lips and stroking labia
    Was Oxford town.

Fond nursemaid of our tender years,
Old Oxford, paradise for queers,
    What delectation
The memory of you inspires,
City of sadly dreaming spires
    And masturbation.

No need for you, Bill, to be pensive.
You spent at Greenhill Comprehensive
    Your adolescence.
At lunchtime meetings in the cloakroom,
The grope-and-tickle, grip-and-stroke room,
    You learned your lessons.

You're now an expert in the chase.
Besides which, coming from a place
    With no sex-bar,
You're maybe capable of seeing
A woman as a human being.
    (I'm told they are.)

So you have got a headstart, matey.
But, more than that, in 1980
    The old regime
In Oxford's past –the change is drastic.
Gone are the ancient ways monastic.
    I'd like to scream!

It's not fair, Bill, you lucky lad.

The thing that nearly drove us mad
   Went grimly on
For generations, firm and fixed.
Then all the colleges went mixed
   When we had gone.

So you'll knock thirty birds per annum,
With "sana mens" have "corpus sanum",
   No empty tears.
But when you're carving up your notches
Think of the pain in all those crotches
   In former years.

*   *   *

Spring and Port Wine

Chris writes: Here is another poem from Barry (written in 1980), preceded by my translation.

tunc interplexis tibi dixi dulcia dextris
   exagerem ut curis lacrima salsa meis,
quamuis sint auersa a me tua terga (locuto
   insulsa insulso uerba parente tuo) –
tunc erat ista ακμη ludi, tunc gaudia summa.
   sed tibi (trux fatum!) basia nulla dedi.
non, sponsae partem quae spectatoribus egit
   illa, meo cordi qualis adesset erat.
dissimulauimus in uero: non talia uerba
   diximus in scaena delineata, nihil
extra. none obseruasti compexibus ultro
   nos spatial inter nos ponere multa datis?
illa tamen nostrum perdulcia uerba duorum
   me libuere – fui non memor huius agens:
annos te tredecim, sedecim tamen atque uiginti
   me uixisse. decem tresque necesse fuit
sic diuidere agentes nos, ut uerus amator
   essem sex quinis: exteriora tua
iuuentute ferenda tibi sunt atque tulisti,
   arteque nos poteras praesuperare tua.
miratum est te tam iuuenem esse, at terror abundans
   me quassit primo tempore (postne tamen?)
ad teneram tractum iuuenem (ut me filia!?!) siccus
   ut solet ad fluuium praecipitare canis
in uita station (nunc confiteamur!) iniqua,
   pons uitae mediae quae nominator, inest –
stat subito ante toras ueluti fur luridus atque

"cede", inquit, "iuuenum de malefacta mihi."
sint tibi nunc mensae potius quam gaudia amoris:
    alea iactetur sufficiatque tibi.
et tu – cui iuueni tua mens uolitabat in illo
    tempore. cui? mihi dic, inuidiaque mea
torquear. actorne? aut pictor qui quattuor annos
    plenos te plures uixerat, ille senex?
aut iubeas aut frigescas illa caritate
    maturo placitam semisenique tua?
mox tuus in ludo genitor fortasse uidebor,
    auctoritae arcens inuidiaque uetans.
at tu me ridens praedulce iocosa, poetae
    uerbis parebis sedula: "carpe diem".
sic solum minimis colorosis forte clamabo
    auxiliis; iuueni basia multa dabis.
non solum seniorem te sed et esse maritum
    me mihi dicendum est. temporibusne nouis
his uni cogitate semper languescere corda
    quaeque puella uiro feminea? atque domo
pulchrum auferre ducem se congratulantibus ultro
    omnibus indeque se gaudia habere? caca!
"ducite, non flagrate, uiri": sic dixerat ille
    tarsius et caelebs, non mala uera sciens.
ducite sed flagrareque nos uideatur, et ille
    hos melius crecit quem sibi terra tenet.
(sic papa noster). amor mortalibus in iuga iactis
    tum quatiens alas auolat inde leues.
felix qui nupsit! lacrimae, deuoluite, tristes!
    quid cum currus equum taedeat atque uiis
praecipitare in bucolicis desiderat ipse
    perque altas uelles fluminque aura uelut
et procul a frenis super aequora lata salire.
    suspicio sequitur rixaque certa domi.
eligat ex mundo praeclaram si quis et empta
    solam constituat semper amare domo
et non intacti perdulcia sentiat unquam
    gaudia ruris, mox taedeat. adde quod et
femineum corpus desuescit; forma tibi illa
    tum placuit, sed nunc tristis abiuit, abest.
pectoral nunc pendent, ruga multa per ora uidetur,
    et maius dominae lingua mouere solet.
ergo per pulchras (dicantur uera!) puellas
    formosasque uiros saepius ardour init.

et sic insanite, omnes, climate, maritae,
    flamma quod anterior mortua nunc sit, eum
appellate caprum putridum, "mensesque uirorum!"
    dicite (caelestes!): lex tamen illa manet
maturum quoque malle uirum placuisse puellae
    (quae lex Postremum praeerit usque Diem).
a sed progenies! memorandum est! denique raptant
    errantes fibros huanitate uiri.
nam compellitur a uitiis auertere se, cum
    in mentem ueniat progenies, et atrox.
et dominae cuicumque est, qui possitque uelitque
    ferre diuina domum commode, habere uirum.
ut natos faciat securos, sordida quamuis
    sit mens, quoquo sunt omnia agenda uiro.
quomodo possumus irriti reperire catharsin?
    tristi furtiuus saepe placebit amor,
(noli, Paule, audire illud), uersusue doloris
    plenos scribamus sintue theatra satis.
has egi res, et multo est melior mihi prima,
    etsi illis allis saepius utar ego.
ultima, dum non sit mandatis corporis aequa,
    tecum, uita,mihi, gauida multa dedit.
iam solum grauida compono grandia uerba
    ex anima atque domum tum uir honestus eo.
omnia tum curae mihi sunt mandata laboris,
    et personarum milia uita parat:
uir dominae curans sum uicinusue benignus,
    cui media aetas est certius illa prope,
interea annorum tredecim insaltare puellam
    ardens (infandum!), lege uetitus amans.
etsi insana mihi arderes, lex saeua uetaret
    tres plures annos; consituere sense
non permittere te mihi te summittere dulce;
    indulgere ueils; lex tamen illa negat.
atque tibi proprias Natura parauit amori
    et pulchras partes – pectoral, crura, sinus.
inque tuo lecto malim esse ut primus amator
    quam superare alios auriga uictor equos
suspiciumque tibi nullum peruenit Hibernum
    qui tibi sit uisus proximus esse Stygi,
etsi grauet eum fragilis natura, propulsum
    esse, decus numeris laudificare tuum.
non eludere te potuit bona Gloria, siue

67

permittent leges siue uetare uelint.
in rebus grauior grauiore in corpore fiam
ardebitque tibi flamma minoris. eris
stella, Ioanna, (actrix annon). nunc stamina uitae
carpe, precor, numquam, stantia. finis adest.

Metre: Elegiacs

English original (John Barry, 1980):

Your hand on mine, the gentle words I said
To comfort you and drive your tears away,
Behind you, looking down upon your head
After your boorish father had his say –
This was the crowning moment of our play,
Its apogee, its highest point of bliss.
Pity it wasn't you I had to kiss.

But no! Unluckily the girl who acted
My fiancée was not my kind of bird.
An act it was, for neither felt attracted.
We played our parts and hardly spoke a word
Off-stage. Perhaps you noticed what occurred –
We quickly put the maximum of inches
Between us on emerging from our clinches.

But I looked forward to our touching scene,
One little thing forgotten in the act:
That I was thirty-six and you thirteen.
Our play demanded that the gulf contract,
So you played six years older than in fact,
I a young blade of thirty. Which was change
Enough to put you just within my range.

You represented on the stage a stage
Of life still not experienced, and outclassed
Us all. Folks were astonished at your age.
I was not just astonished but aghast –
Now the first time (though maybe not the last!)
Attracted like a thirsty hound to water
By someone who could really be my daughter.

Yes, it's a nasty moment in our lives,
That watershed we call the mid-life crisis!
Like a grim-hooded robber it arrives,
Says, "Stick 'em up. Hand over young men's vices.
Console yourself with tea and cake and ices
For what you're losing underneath the belly.
Goodbye, the joys of love. Turn on the telly."

And you meanwhile, I wonder who you found
To fantasize on – tell me, make me green!
Another actor? The chap who did the sound.
Prepared the props, or helped to paint the scene
(Boasting the ripe old age of seventeen)?
Would you be flattered or a little haughty
At having an admirer touching forty?

Perhaps next time I'll actually play your father
Jealously urging caution and restraint,
While you just thumb your nose at me and gather
Rosebuds, like the poet said, before they faint.
I'll not require much make-up: a little paint
To line the brow, powder for extra grey.
You'll hug your lover while I rant away.

An admirer touching forty, a man with wife!
Do young girls dream still, in these liberated
Permissive days that love will last for life?
That every Sue and Mirabel is fated
To meet her Mr. Right and then get mated
To sound of bells and sermons, jokes and laughter,
The happy ever after? Nothing dafter.

"It's best to marry, not burn", St. Paul opined,
Who never married, and the truth would sicken him.
"Marry and burn" is what we mostly find.
As flowers grow best when we refrain from pickin' 'em
(Thus said our English Pope whose Rome was Twickenham).
"Love, free as air, at sight of human tie
Spreads his light wings and out the window flies."

Ah, the enchantment, ah, the bliss of marriage!'
The thing's enough to bring on tears or stitches.
What when the horse gets tired of the carriage,
The trot along suburban lanes, and itches
To gallop free, jump over gates and ditches,
Romp on the open fields without constriction?
It's a sure way to acuse domestic friction.

To choose one comely maid from all the store
Available, and never look at more.
Purchase your little house and shut the door.
Never again, never again explore
Another's person, feel your spirit soar
On sighting fields not galloped in before –
Fine for six months (six years?), then what a bore.

And there's another thing besides monotony,
That o so very quickly women flag.
That shape you loved, now look, she hasn't got any.
Those winsome little tits begin to sag.
Crows leave their tracks. Add, that wives tend to nag.
Let's admit candidly, girls sweet and luscious
Are far more likely to give fellows crushes.

So face it, ladies, though you rant and curse,
Missing the urgent passion that once was,
Call him "dirty old man" or – even worse –
Make snide remarks on the male menopause,
It's futile! This most basic of life's laws
Will last when we've abolished dukes and earls –
That older men are drawn to younger girls.

Ah, but the children! Society can't function
If men go gallivanting. There's the rub.

The most unfeeling brute must have compulsion
Considering the little ones. A wife needs hub
To earn the wherewithal to buy the grub.
For sake of offspring, though his thoughts lack purity,
A man must do his best to bring security.

Frustrated thus, how can we find catharsis?
A love-affair conducted with discretion
Does wonders for morale, though Paul of Tarsus
To human frailty made no concession.
Or we can try a less direct concession-
Compose lugubrious verse in lonely attics,
Or else resort to amateur dramatics.

I've done all three and much prefer the first.
More often, though, the others must suffice.
The last, although it mightn't slake the thirst,
With sweet thirteen was very very nice.
In this lean time, alas, my only vice
Is the middle one: in rollicking Rhyme Royal
To express my angst – and then be tamely loyal.

And thus "catharsed" I face my daily labour –
The roles I have to follow on life's stage:
Considerate husband, inoffensive neighbour,
The family man approaching middle age;
Smooth words for all, while inwardly I rage
To pounce upon my love-child like an eagle –
A thing not just immoral but illegal,

Illegal, even if you should consent!
Only thirteen, you've three years yet to go.
Your warm responsive answer is not meant,
At least some ancient clerks decided so,
And while you clamour yes, the law says no,
Though for man's pleasure splendidly equipped,
Already so well-breasted, -legged and –hipped.

I'd like to be the first man in your bed
Far more than play for Leeds and get a hat-trick.
There's not the least suspicion in your head
That someone who to you seems geriatric,
Who comes from Ireland (although not called Patrick)
Was moved, despite short breath and creaky joints,
To celebrate in verse your finer points.

Nothing will stop you on your path of glory
Whether or not respecting the law's ban.
While I get bald and fat, become a Tory,
You'll rev the engine of some younger man.
On stage, in life, you'll be a star, Joann.
Now seize the bloom, so fast, so fast it goes.
With that original remark, I'll close.

*   *   *

70

Catherine B. Krause

Catherine B. Krause has a Bachelor of Science in Computer Science from Dickinson College and hopes to one day go back to school to study philology. Her poetry has been published in English, Esperanto, Interlingua and Latin, there have been talks of soon publishing her translated poetry in Ido and her prose has been published in English and Esperanto. She created the metrical form of the 'quincouplet', which she has here Hellenised as 'pentedistichon'. She became interested in Latin verse as part of a secret desire to become the most influential Jewish writer in Latin since Josephus.

Tres Haicua

Catherine writes: Three haiku, both in Latin and in English.

(1)

> *adhuc mane est hic.*
> *uelamen ecce nigrum*
> *noctis se auferat.*

> It's still early here.
> Behold, the black veil of night
> lifts itself away.

(2)

> *coniuit Deus*
> *et uno eruptione*
> *nata omnia sunt.*

> The Creator blinked
> and a single eruption
> gave birth to all things.

(3)

> *dum nocte ambulo,*
> *uiam mihi nix lustrat,*
> *hiberni ancilla.*

> As I walk at night
> my way is lighted by snow,
> the winter servant.

*   *   *

Carmen

Catherine writes: I wrote this as a 'persona poem', from the perspective of a jealous boyfriend dating a language learner.

mea amica dextera in lingua est
tamen nuper locuta non mihi sed barbaris...

Translation:

My girlfriend is skilled with her tongue,
although lately she has spoken, not to me, but to barbarians...

*   *   *

Duo Pentedisticha

Catherine writes: Although "pentedistichon" is not as clever a name as "quincouplet," I prefer to use declinable words whenever possible, and to follow the custom of some other Latin writers not to mix two languages within the same word (hence "pentedistichon" vs. "quindistichon"). That said, tradition almost always comes first, so "Cain" remains "Cain."

Malum

plenissima colorum
folia moritura sunt.

The leaves most full of colours are about to die.

Pacifismus

Cain quoque
sub Deo fuit.

Even Cain was under God's protection.

*   *   *

Jan Křesadlo

Jan Křesadlo was the primary pseudonym of Václav Jaroslav Karel Pinkava (1926-1995), a Czech psychologist, polymath and polyglot, composer, mathematician, prizewinning novelist and poet. An anti-communist, Pinkava emigrated to Britain with his wife and four children following the 1968 invasion of Czechoslovakia. He worked as a clinical psychologist until his early retirement in 1982, when he turned to full-time writing.

Divisio Palaeontologica Musei Historiae Naturalis Londinensis

Václav Pinkava writes: My father was very much a polyglot, and wrote poems in various languages, including Latin. This one from a collection published in the 1980s resonates with one by the editor of this journal [*Dinosauria*], as it is set in the London Natural History Museum. Here among all the exhibits of extinct species we find a *memento mori* for the human visitors, who are all destined to go the same way.

Dinornis elephantopus
altus uiginti cubitus,
Batrachorhynchus clauiceps
quem mirans perturbatur plebs,
minatur rostro tricorni
Trinacromerum Osborni.
est Allosaurus infimus
est atque Struthiomimus,
Gorgosaurus, Diplodocus,
est furiosus Helocus,
Procompsognathus monstrosus
ac Spinosaurus spinosus,
est Stegosaurus scutifer
sicut creasset Lucifer,
est cornu Triceratopis,
est pes cuiusdam inopis,
iungitur Tetralophodon,
adest et Iguanodon,
qui osseo in nemore
enormi gaudet femore,
est atque alia fera,

et cetera, et cetera,
quae ego neque narrare
scio, nec enumerare:
sunt crura, pelues, ischia,
sunt maxillae, sunt bracchia,
sunt phalanges, tarsalia,
sunt grandia carpalia,
sunt dentes quasi gladii,
sunt ulnae atque radii
similes truncis arborum.
et minimum os carporum
uix subleues in manibus,
quod tamen in hominibus
est sicut granum minutum:
nonnullum rostrum acutum
confraternatur cornibus
unguibus atque dentibus:
periculosa portenta
et illorum armamenta
hic habent coemeterium.
iam dormit Dinotherium
quod attamen horribile
simul erat peribile:
omnia quae hic uidere
potes, cuncta periere:
et tu peribis misere,
neque poteris manere.
manebit solum crus et dens
sub scripto: HOMO SAPIENS.

Metre: Rhythmic

Translation:

Dinornis elephantopus twenty cubits high, Batrachorhynchus claviceps, admired by awestruck people, threatened by the trident beak of Trinacromerum Osborni. Allosaurus the base and Struthiomimus, Gorgosaurus, Diplodocus, Helocus the furious, Procompsognathus the monstrous Spinosaurus the thorny, Stegosaurus the digger just as if created by Lucifer, the horned Triceratops, some foot of some unfortunate beast joins Tetralophodon, and Iguanodon is here, who, in this forest of bones enjoys the most enormous thigh, and other wild creatures, and so on and so forth, that I do not know how to describe, but not forgetting: there are legs, pelvises, hips, jawbones, arms, there are the fingers, tarsals great carpals, the swordlike teeth, the radii and ulnas like the trunks of trees. And the smallest mouth bones hardly fit in the hands, given that a man by comparison is as small as a grain; some sharp beaks keep company with horns claws and teeth; dangerous

74

monsters and their armaments, here have their cemetery. Therein already sleeps the Dinotherium, quod however horrible was also perishable. All that you are able to see here likewise shall perish, and you too will perish miserably, unable to remain. The only keepsakes being a leg and a tooth and the inscription: Homo Sapiens.

*   *   *

Raul Lavalle

Raul Lavalle (latine *Radulfus Bonaerensis*) was born in 1953 and teaches Latin in Buenos Aires, Argentina. He wrote several articles, translated some Greek and Latin texts and has a blog devoted to literature (www.litterulae.blogspot.com).

Laus Bacchi

Raul writes: I once entered this *carmen* in a Latin poetry competition, not because I expected to win but because I wanted to see my name alongside the other learned entrants. It is written in free verse, a kind of 'visual metric', *ut ita dicam*, by which I mean the verses have the same or similar extension, if you read them. For instance:

laudo te, doctissime Marce,
quia res hodiernas Latinas
in Anglia, maris imperatrice,
optime colis.

Sometimes the last verse is a sort of *pie quebrado*, a kind of Adonic. I write 'my way'.

Lenaee, audi me benignus:
non sum Tyrrhenus nauta.
salue, polyonyme daemon!
Omnes tuas gestas laudant
populi, quas in Asia et dulci
in Europa et in Aethiopum
tractibus necnon in India,
mirabiliorum terra, peregisti.
at praedulce nobis nectar
est, quod hominum generi
cottidie das. quam tristes
essemus, si fortem uitis
sucum nos non libaremus!
uino curas nostras leuamus;
uino deitatem pura mente
ueneramur; saliares dapes
uino mitigamus; uino sermo
Socraticus madet, ut subtili
sophorum uoce gaudeamus;
uino corporum constitutio
roboratur et puellas amare
discimus; uino obliuionem
malorum capimus amorum.

ueni, Euhan, mentes uisita
tuorum fidelium!

Metre: Free verse

Translation:

> Lenaeus, hear me tenderly:
> I'm not a Tyrrhenian mariner.
> Hail, god with a lot of names!
> All nations praise your deeds,
> which in Asia and in the sweet
> Europe, in realms of Ethiopians
> and in India, land of marvelous
> things and miracles, you've done.
> Extremely sweet is the nectar
> you give to the human races
> every day. How sad we should be,
> if we couldn't taste the strong
> juice that the grapes produce.
> With wine we calm our pains;
> with wine God in pure souls
> pray; the banquets of the *Salii*
> we relief with wine; wine needs
> the Socratic conversation,
> to perceive the wise men's
> voices; with wine our bodies
> become stronger and we learn
> to love the girls; oblivion of our
> unhappy loves in wine we obtain.
> Come, *Euhan*, and visit the spirit
> of your faithfuls.

*   *   *

Uxorí In Italiam Iter Facientí

Raul writes: This little poem is written in trochaic accentual verse. Of course, as it's possible to see, my verses have a lot of poetic licences, in accents and in syllables. I beg pardon for my bad "Spanish" English, a language anyhow that I love; of course, for my *delirum sermonem Latinum*. The word *Latinoamnesicanus* of course has a pun. In the radio a journalist used to criticize in that way the forgetful character of Latin American people. I feel that we Argentineans find it very difficult to learn from our mistakes.

ualeas, uxor mea pulchra,
quae reuises Italiam.
miraberis monumenta,
quae gloriosa excellunt.
sed –pro dolor! – Italicus
uir te a me auferet.

77

certe illi sunt diuitiae
et me tenet paupertas;
illi pulchro est media aetas,
nos opprimit senectus;
sum Latinoamnesicanus,
optimatium est unus.
quoquo modo abi, uxor,
sed memoriam mei habeas:
etsi multi sunt meliores
est in me fidelitas.
etiam dei terras uisitant:
et tu in brachia reuenias.
(uxor mea iter fecit 22 Ian. 2014.)

Metre: Rhythmic Trochaic

Translation: Good bye, my beautiful wife,

Who will travel to Italy.
You'll admire the monuments
Which are full of glory.
But –oh pain!– an Italian
Will deprive me of your love.
Sure he's very rich
And I am so poor;
He is nice and middle aged
And I am very old;
I'm from Latin America
And he belongs to nobility.
Anyhow, good bye, my wife,
But, please, remember me:
It's true a lot of men are better
Than me, but loyalty is in me.
The gods sometimes visit the Earth:
You too, I pray, return to me.

(My wife travelled on 22 Jan. 2014)

*   *   *

John Lee

John Lee read Classics in Queensland and at Oxford many years ago and later taught Philosophy in Newcastle, New South Wales. He began writing Latin verse in retirement.

Per Nauem ad Byzantios (ii)

John Lee writes: This is a revision of *Per Nauem ad Byzantios*, my earlier Latin version of W.B. Yeats's poem 'Sailing to Byzantium' (*Vates*, Issue 3, 2011). Most of the alterations are in the third and fourth stanzas. In line 24 I have put *diuom fabrica* for Yeats's 'artifice of eternity', which I take to be the product of art which is transcendent, i.e. outside space and time and in the eternal realm of divine or quasi-divine beings such as the sages. *Fabrica* can also mean 'smithy', which brings to mind the laboratory of the Craftsman of Plato's *Timaeus*.

> non senibus terra est quae nunc delectat amantes,
> quae iuuenes iungit pinnigeras et aues,
> qua salit et salmo rutilans et scomber abundat
> et calido laudat tempore quisque suos,
> exanimos genitosque sui qua quisque celebrat,
> qua pereunt omnes dum pereuntque canunt:
> sic animos cepit sensusque canora uoluptas
> mentis ut omittant paene perennis opus.
>
> nil nisi uile senex, baculum quod trita lacerna
> panniculis uestit, ni prius ipse canat.
> heus! animus plaudat, canat usque et uociferetur,
> quemque canat pannum lingua uetusta togae;
> nec schola cantorum est, animus nisi pulchra requirat
> quae pia splendoris sunt monumenta sui;
> huc igitur uectus sacratae protinus urbis
> Constantinopolis trans mare fana peto.
>
> sicut in aurato muro fulgente lapillis
> qui Domini sancto statis in igne magi,
> uos precor, in gyrum rapidum mihi uertite motum:
> carmina sic animam uestra docete meam.
> heu! moriens animal cum corde cupidine iunctum est,
> nec nouit se cor quod regit atra uenus;
> quod manet in me tam penitus consumite cordis
> ut mihi sit diuom fabrica sola domus.

haec mihi si superi naturae uincla resoluant
talia non rursus tum mihi membra legam,
sed ueluti uitra sint quae conflant aurea Graeci
tenuis caute lamina tunsa fabris,
languida ne Caesar declinet lumina somno
uel sedeat ramis in nitidis ut auis
aurea quae cantet dominis Byzantiacorum
praeterita et quod iam praeterit et quod erit.

Metre: Elegiacs

Translation:

That is no country for old men, that now delights lovers and joins in bliss young folk and birds of the air, where red-glowing salmon leap and mackerel abound, where in summer each extols his own, making much of newborn and dead, and where all die with a song on their lips; so captive are the mind and the senses to its seductive strains that the achievement of enduring intellect is barely noticed.

An aged man is but a paltry thing, a walking-stick covered in rags by a worn cloak, unless first he sings. Hey there, let the mind clap, let it go on singing and crying out; let the aged tongue sing for every patch on its dress; nor is there a singing school, unless the mind goes in search of fine things, of the reverent monuments to its own magnificence; so I have come here, across the sea without delay, seeking the shrines of the hallowed city of Byzantium.

O sages standing in God's holy fire, as in a gilded wall gleaming with bright mosaic tiles, I beg you, turn your whirling dance into a spiral – in this way teach my soul your songs. Alas, a dying animal has been joined by desire to [this] heart which, ruled by morbid indulgence, is a stranger to itself. Consume so thoroughly what remains of it that the artifice of divine beings is my only abode.

Were the powers above to unloose for me these bonds of nature, I should not choose again such members; rather let them be like the gold enamel that Greeks fire in their furnaces and the fine leaf hammered by careful goldsmiths to keep an Emperor's tired eyes from closing in sleep, or have a golden bird sit amid gleaming branches to sing to nobles of Byzantium of what has passed, what is now passing and what will be.

Original: *Sailing to Byzantium* (W.B. Yeats)

> That is no country for old men. The young
> In one another's arms, birds in the trees
> —Those dying generations—at their song,
> The salmon-falls, the mackerel-crowded seas,
> Fish, flesh, or fowl, commend all summer long
> Whatever is begotten, born, and dies.
> Caught in that sensual music all neglect
> Monuments of unageing intellect.
>
> An aged man is but a paltry thing,
> A tattered coat upon a stick, unless
> Soul clap its hands and sing, and louder sing
> For every tatter in its mortal dress,
> Nor is there singing school but studying
> Monuments of its own magnificence;

And therefore I have sailed the seas and come
To the holy city of Byzantium.

O sages standing in God's holy fire
As in the gold mosaic of a wall,
Come from the holy fire, perne in a gyre,
And be the singing-masters of my soul.
Consume my heart away; sick with desire
And fastened to a dying animal
It knows not what it is; and gather me
Into the artifice of eternity.

Once out of nature I shall never take
My bodily form from any natural thing,
But such a form as Grecian goldsmiths make
Of hammered gold and gold enamelling
To keep a drowsy Emperor awake;
Or set upon a golden bough to sing
To lords and ladies of Byzantium
Of what is past, or passing, or to come.

*   *   *

Frank Lelièvre

Frank Lelièvre was Professor of Classics at Magee College in Londonderry and then at the University of Ulster in Coleraine. He published three volumes, subtitled 'Latin poems in various metres', which include both translations from English originals and new Latin poems. These are *Across Bin Brook* (1992, with H.H. Huxley), *Serus Vindemitor* (1995) and *Rarae Uvae* (2009).This poem appeared in the very first issue of *Vates*, before Prof Lelièvre's death in 2012.

For A Beginner

The editor writes: In this poem Frank Lelièvre offers some words of advice for all those just beginning to write Latin verse. It is taken with the author's kind permission from *Across Bin Brook* (1992), a collection of poems by Professor Lelièvre and H. H. Huxley. It was also reprinted with the translation below in the editor's *Britannica Latina: 2000 Years of British Latin* (2009).

> *perstare, credo, Musa suos iubet,*
> *utcumque chordis dulcisonos negat*
> *   cantus et, exoptata quamuis,*
> *   peruigilem refugit lucernam.*
>
> *nascentis ipso germine flos rosae*
> *celatur: ignem dura tegit silex:*
> *   et terra fulgorem smaragdi*
> *   condidit interiore saxo.*
>
> *at pertinacem, sera licet, uirum*
> *ditare gaudet: non silicis latet*
> *   scintilla percussae, nec omni*
> *   tempore flos Veneris moratur.*
> *tu perge tantum, namque potes, modis*
> *uerba experiri conuenientia.*
> *   te Musa quaerentem docebit*
> *   mente noua reparare carmen.*

Metre: Alcaics

Editor's Translation:

> The Muse, I reckon, tells her own followers to keep trying, even though she withholds sweet-sounding songs from our strings and, however much she is longed for, shuns our night-long labours. The flower of the

growing rose is concealed in its own bud: hard flint hides the fire: and the Earth kept locked away in its inmost rock the brilliance of the emerald. But she rejoices, although tardily, to enrich the tenacious man: the spark of a struck flint is not hidden, nor is the flower of Love delayed for all time. You, carry on at any rate experimenting, for indeed you can, with harmonious words in your measures. The Muse will teach you while you are learning to amend your song with new understanding.

*   *   *

Thomas Lindner

Thomas Lindner lives in Austria and is Professor of Comparative Philology in the Linguistics Department at the University of Salzburg. He is also a Member of the Austrian Academy of Sciences. His research interests focus mainly on the classical languages. He has published several books and many articles on Latin, Greek, and Indo-European linguistics.

A Plea for Consolation

Thomas writes: I wrote this poem in 1987, when still a teenager, suffering from tedium and eagerly waiting for inspiration from my Muse. In the 1990s, I compiled some 60 poems of mine and published them in a collection named *Lyra Latina* (1st edition, Vienna 1994; 2nd edition: Vienna 1997). Finally, a critical edition with a textual apparatus and metrical analyses appeared in 2012.

> *descende caelo, Musa, ueni mihi,*
> *ueni poetae, qui miser in toro*
>   *iacet nec ullis adiuuatur*
>   *deliciis et hebet uigore.*
>
> *succurre tandem neue neges mihi*
> *tam dulce donum! deprecor: acria*
>   *mutes odoro nectare inde,*
>   *ambrosiaque fruar suavi.*

(Lyra Latina, carmen XXII)

Metre: Alcaics

Translation:

Descend from heaven, oh Muse, and come to me, to the poet, who lies in bed unhappily, lacks strength and cannot draw comfort by any delights. Finally help and do not deny me your lovely gifts. I beseech you: from now on do exchange the exasperation with redolent nectar, and I will enjoy your sweet ambrosia.

*   *   *

Andreas Lovaniensis

Andreas Lovaniensis is the *nom de plume* of Andy Peetermans, who was born in 1990 in the city of Lier (Belgium). He started studying Latin and Italian at the university of Leuven in 2008; in 2013, Ancient Greek followed. He has written small amounts of publishable poetry in Esperanto, Dutch and Latin.

A Quincouplet

Andreas writes: The haiku-like form of the quincouplet was suggested to me by its creator, the American poet Catherine B. Krause (who later started writing Latin poetry). As she explained, "The rules of a quincouplet, or quin, are simple. There are two lines, with two words on the first line and three words on the second. It need not have a title, but if it does, the title must consist of only one word. The title can be used for any purpose except as the first word of a sentence continued by the poem." In the following week, I produced what were probably the first two quins in the history of Latin poetry, the first of which I would like to present here. *Vulnerasti* is an experiment in intertextuality-assisted brevity: while its title points towards the biblical *Canticum Canticorum* (4:9 "Vulnerasti cor meum..."), the inclusion of the word *domina* opens a doorway to the world of Roman elegiac poetry. It also plays with multiplicity and vagueness of meaning when the context is underspecified.

Vulnerasti

> *dormiente domina*
> *arcana lustrat versibus.*

Metre: Quincouplet

Translation: *Wounded.*

> While his lady sleeps, he *lustrat** the *arcana*** by means of verses.

> [**lustrat*: illuminates, encircles, examines, purifies.
> ***arcana*: hidden/intimate/private feelings, secrets.]

*   *   *

Epigrammata Amatoria

Andreas writes: *De Alacri puella*, which I wrote in the late spring of 2012 for a fellow Latin student after hearing her sing as a part of the university choir, was my first attempt at writing classical metrical verse. *Ad Floram puellam*, written in May 2013, was originally accompanied by an interpretation in Dutch. Firstly because the girl I wrote it for – who had a kind of fuchsia named after her by her grandfather, which explains the flower references – didn't read Latin very well; secondly because *conflauens* (which might mean 'thoroughly and harmoniously exhuming blondness') is not in the dictionary. There is a metrical license in the beginning of the third verse, for which I hope to be forgiven by more critical readers. The loves of which these poems speak were not so much lost as never really born. These Latin verses are all that remains of them – or all that ever was.

De Alacri puella

> cantat amata Alacris philomela carmina digna –
> corda ardore implens uocula blandula alit.

Ad Floram puellam

> quam pulchras conflauentis hyacinthea praeter
> lumina laeta geris, bellula Flora, comas;
> uirgo uenusta, mane, flos florum, floscule, mecum –
> quem conflasti in me ne renuas animum!

Metre: Elegiacs

Translations: *Of Alacris.*

> My beloved Alacris sings songs worthy of a nightingale – her sweet little voice nourishes my heart, filling it with ardor.

> *To Flora.*

> What beautiful hair of most harmonious blondeness you have, comely little Flora, besides your hyacinth-blue eyes full of joy; stay with me, fair maiden, flower of flowers, sweet flower – may you not refuse the *animus** you sparked in me! [*animus*: feeling, courage, life force, desire.]

*   *   *

Birthday Verses

Andreas writes: The poem, which I wrote on the seventh of June 2015, was originally accompanied by this:

    QVOD QVINQVIES QVINOS
    ANDREAS AMICVS ANNOS
    CHRISTOPHORO CECINIT COMITI COMI CARMEN
    NVPER NATO

Which becomes more readable by switching around the word order: *quod carmen Christophoro comiti comi, quinquies quinos annos nato, nuper cecinit Andreas amicus*; which is to say I wrote this poem for my kind friend Christophe, who turned twenty-five.

uiuas, Christophore, atque dona fati
iam fiant tibi copiosa amico –
nam morans Venus et diu morata
te comem coluisse non uidetur –
sit comi dea, amice, comior – hoc sit
munus Cypridis Andreae poetae.

Metre: Phalaecian hendecasyllables

Translation:

> May you live, Christophe, and may the gifts of fate from now on come to you in great numbers, my friend. Indeed, it seems a foolish Venus, keeping you waiting for a long time, has not kept you in honor, kind though you are. May the Cyprian goddess be kind to you, who are yourself kind, my friend. May that be her gift to Andy who's writing this poem.

*   *   *

Michelangelo Macchiarella

Michelangelo Macchiarella had a dream in Los Angeles last night wherein he looked at himself in the mirror and said, "I am just a composite of everything I do." Awaking this morning, he reclines on the patio, shuts his eyes to the sun and drinks his coffee; he speaks aloud, "That just means that I am nothing."

Quattuor Poemata

(1) Text Messages

Michelangelo writes: I wrote this in San Francisco – the fog had seeped inward.

> *tibi,*
> *o insomnis puella,*
> *ipsi dedi meum cor;*
> *tum, amor noster fuit magnus,*
> *nunc, quid est?*
> *sicut meum cor:*
> *et nihil et nullumque:*
> *inane atque uacuom*
> *... sterile.*

Metre: Free verse

Translation:

> I read her this once;
> She said she didn't understand
> And that I should go.

*   *   *

(2) Verses to be Sung

A constant struggle against ennui ensues.

> *uerso saepe de me morituro*
> *aegrus for' opinor*
> *uomitus miser*
> *uenter se uersat -*
> *eg' aegrebo*
> *uerso me lapsare*
> *hac doct' ex uita -*

aeger aegrebo

Metre: Free verse
Translation:

> Oft view
> Myself I –
> It's not loathing
> See I self
> It's me see
> Sick I –
> To far gone
> Too
> "Ayuda me."

*　　*　　*

(3) Yellow is the Colour of Panorama City

I never did understand why she called – why she was crying.

> *fortasse parum dixi.*
> *'fortasse,' inquit, 'dixti mature,' ipsa.*
> *Urbs Angelum non est stellis.*
> *'Urbs,' inquit, 'Angelum stellas non habet,' ipsa.*

> *parua uerba tam inter sese bene coniecta*

Metre: Free verse
Translation:

> Perhaps I spoke too little.
> "Perhaps you spoke too soon," she said.
> Los Angeles is a starless city.
> "Los Angeles hasn't any stars," she said.

> In the end they were all just little words so nicely placed together

*　　*　　*

(4) YouTube

I can't stop watching her.

> *media nocte*
> *et defessus*
> *iterum ego.*
> *media nocte*

et consilium
habeo animo -
idem ego.
media nocte
iam praetereunte
tantum tempus
sedeo
caput in manu
et cogito
de quadam:

ipsam roseos in parietem
infibulantem chartae flores
in lecticula hoc perfecto
accumbentem
cruentos
scrutantem
percipio.

A labiis respirat -
et
et
claudit
cameram.

Coda: *Quid fieri potest ut gerrat bene me absente?*

Metre: Free verse

Translation:

She sits and plays her guitar in the nude
She smokes a few cigarettes
She cries a lot and I don't know where she lives anymore.

I didn't reply when she asked to see me before she left.

She is - and the while
She delicately pins her paper flowers to the wall.

I never answer but I read everything she writes me.
I never pick-up but I listen to everything she leaves me.
I never see her but I know she wears my old P.E. shirt and -
I like it.
Coda: Am I sick to think that she can't be happy without me?

*   *   *

Jonathan Meyer

Jonathan Meyer is a Ph.D. student in Classics at Johns Hopkins University, where he studies neo-Latin literature. Recent academic peregrinations include a year spent at the American School of Classical Studies in Athens, Greece, as well as a six-month fellowship at the Ludwig Boltzmann Institute for Neo-Latin Studies in Innsbruck, Austria, where he worked on eighteenth-century neo-Latin novels written in the Habsburg empire. Apart from being an aspiring Latin versifier, Jonathan is a proponent of spoken Latin. He earned a Masters degree in the active Latin program at the University of Kentucky, and he is also an instructor for "Living Latin in Rome," a summer program for university students organized by the Paideia Institute for Humanistic Study.

Cyclops

Jonathan writes: Translation from Greek into Latin was considered a highly useful exercise by the ancients, particularly in the field of rhetoric (cf. Quintilian, *Inst.* 10.5.2-3; Pliny, *Ep.* 7.9.2). Roman poets also honed their craft by translating and adapting Greek models; Catullus 51 (*Ille mi par esse deo uidetur*), which reworks a famous poem by Sappho, is a particularly celebrated example. For my first foray into Latin verse—*quod sectanda puto ueterum uestigia uatum*, à la Lovato de' Lovati—I took as my muse Theocritus' *Idyll* 11, a poem that was imitated by Vergil and Ovid, among others. My version quarries bits and pieces of Theocritus' Greek original; occasionally I translate *ad litteram*, more often *ad sensum*, and sometimes I depart from the Greek text altogether.

> *fessos cunctorum somnus deuinxerat artus:*
> *euigilans sed crebra trahit suspiria Cyclops,*
> *deperiebat enim Galateam maestus amore,*
> *unicum et obscuras conuertens lumen ad undas*
> *"Cur, crudelis," ait, "cur me contemnis amantem?*
> *rupibus asperior, leuior tu sidere noctis,*
> *sollicito, quod laeta secas, incertior alto:*
> *te pelago mergis, quotiens ad litus adiui,*
> *ex pelago surgis, quotiens a litore abiui,*
> *effugit et uelut agna lupum tremefacta sequentem,*
> *sic das terga fugae. nec me latet, alma puella,*
> *cur fugias: ingens odio est medio orbis in ore,*
> *hirsutumque horres, quod ab aure tetendit ad aurem,*
> *grande supercilium. quales sed cumque uidemur,*
> *balantes sunt mille mihi, sunt mille capellae,*
> *compescuntque sitim niueo spumantia lacte*
> *pocula: nec sitiensue Canis gelidiue Bootes*
> *mellis conspiciunt calathos redolentis inanes.*

umbratum patulis, mea tecta, cupressibus antrum
quid referam? numquis tam dulciter aequora ponti
incolit? o si me genetrix peperisset amata
squamis obtectum! celeri tua limina cursu
per fluuios peterem, cum calthis lilia portans,
tangerem et ore manum, si non os ore liceret,
terraque cur odio tibi sit, cur marmora cordi,
tandem perciperem. mens, ah!, mens integra quondam
quo uolitat? calathos, Cyclops, age, uimine texe,
praesentem mulge: quid enim fugitiua sequenda est?
fulgida conuexum decorant quot sidera caelum,
pisces quot sub aquis remigant, totidem Galateae."

Metre: Hexameters

Translation: *Cyclops*

Sleep had bound fast the wearied limbs of all, but wide awake the Cyclops heaved frequent sighs; for he, dejected, was dying in love for Galatea. Turning his single eye to the dark waves, he said, "Why, cruel one, why do you spurn me, though I love you? Harsher than the crags, more fickle than the moon, more inconstant than the restless deep, which you happily swim through: you plunge into the sea whenever I approach the shore, you rise from the sea whenever I leave the shore, and as a trembling lamb flees a pursuing wolf, so you turn your back in flight. Nor, kind girl, does the reason for your flight escape me: you hate the massive eye in the middle of my face, and you bristle at the large, shaggy eyebrow that stretches from ear to ear. But whatever my appearance, I have a thousand bleating sheep and a thousand goats, and cups brimming with snow-white milk slake my thirst; nor do the thirsty Dog or frozen Bootes look upon bowls empty of fragrant honey. Why should I mention the cave, my home, shaded by spreading cypresses? Does anyone lead so pleasant a life in the sea? If only my beloved mother had given birth to me covered with scales! I would make for your threshold in swift course through the water, bringing lilies and marigold, and I would kiss your hand, if I were not allowed to kiss your mouth, and at last I would understand why you hate the land and love the sea. My mind, ah!, my mind, once unimpaired: where does it fly? Come, Cyclops, weave your baskets of twig. Milk what is at hand: why must she who flees be followed? As many are the bright stars that grace the vault of heaven, as many are the fish that row beneath the waters, there are so many Galateas."

*   *   *

De Vulpe et Leone Aegroto

Jonathan writes: This poem is a Latin rendition of the fable of the fox and the sick lion, adapted from the Greek version of Babrius (103). Plato refers to the fable in the *First Alcibiades* (123a), attributing it to Aesop. There is a further allusion in Horace's *Epistles* (1.1.70-75). Like Phaedrus, Babrius writes his

Greek fables in iambics; I have preferred elegiac couplets in the manner of Avianus.

rex nemorum longis fuerat confectus ab annis,
  nec potuit praedam prendere, ut ante, leo.
conuexo ergo ingens extendit corpus in antro,
  crudeli simulans membra dolore premi:
fictaque commiscet lacrimis suspiria fictis,
  astuto et querulos edidit ore sonos.
garrula ad umbriferas brutorum Fama latebras
  uenerat, et plorans bestia quaeque gemit:
"Di melius! rex, heu!, morbo cruciatur acerbo!"
  sic ait, utque aegrum mulceat, antra subit.
iam ceruumque caprumque leo leporemque lupumque
  ceperat, exstinguens absque labore famem,
ad lustrum cum forte uenit cautissima uulpes,
  atque "Satin' salue, maxime rector?" ait.
cui "Sis salua," refert, "o maxima gloria siluae!
  cur non aduenies, meque tuere procul?
huc ades, ut uario curas sermone repellas,
  desque mihi, mox qui sim moriturus, opem."
illa "Velim fortuna" inquit "meliore fruaris!
  at mihi fert animus corripuisse fugam.
nam me, quae aspicio, faciunt uestigia cautam:
  omnia adire cauum, nulla redire patet."
felix, quem potuit clades aliena docere,
  prouidus ut casum uitet et ipse suum.

Metre: Elegiacs

Translation: *The Fox and the Sick Lion*

A lion, the king of the jungle, had been worn out by long years, and he was not able to catch prey as before. So he stretched out his enormous body in a vaulted cave, pretending that his limbs were afflicted with intense pain; and he mingled feigned sighs with feigned tears, and brought forth sounds of complaint from his cunning mouth. Talkative Rumor came to the shady lairs of the animals, and each creature cried out in tears, "Heaven forbid! The king, alas, is being tormented by a harsh malady!" Thus spoke each creature, and entered the cave to soothe the invalid. The lion had already seized a stag and a goat and a hare and a wolf, satisfying his hunger without difficulty, when by chance a wary fox came to his den and said, "Is everything all right, great ruler?" He replied to her, "Greetings, great glory of the forest! Why won't you come closer? Why do you gaze at me from afar? Come here, so that you can relieve my cares with varied conversation and give me help, since I am going to die soon." The fox said, "May you enjoy better fortune! But I am inclined to depart. For the tracks which I see make me wary: it is clear that all the tracks enter the cave, but none come out." Fortunate are they

93

who can learn from the disaster of others, so that, with foresight, they can avoid their own calamity.

*   *   *

Basia Enumerata

Jonathan writes: No Latin poet celebrated the kiss more famously than Catullus, but it was Janus Secundus (1511-1536), the Dutch neo-Latin poet and prodigy, who offered the most elaborate—and perhaps most brilliant—treatment of the theme. Secundus' best known work, the *Basia*, is a cycle of nineteen brief poems written in a variety of meters, each one dwelling lovingly on the topic of the kiss. The seventh *Basium* in the cycle (*Centum basia centies*) reveals most clearly the Catullan inspiration for the work, playing as it does on the theme of "counting kisses" after the manner of Catullus 5 (*Viuamus, mea Lesbia, atque amemus*) and 7 (*Quaeris quot mihi basiationes*). The poem below is a tribute to the *doctus poeta* and his Renaissance reincarnation.

> *dulcia uesani poscunt quot basia uates!*
>   *innumera enumerant: post ea plura petunt!*
> *nam tu mille, dein centum, deinde altera mille*
>   *basia, dein centum, docte Catulle, rogas –*
> *nec iam finis adest – dein milleque et altera centum*
>   *adiungis: summam quis reputare potest?*
> *heu! opus est abaco. numerantur milia terna,*
>   *ter centum. sunt haec satque superque uiro?*
> *ille negat: "Lybico quot sunt in litore harenae,*
>   *quot stellae, tot erunt satque superque mihi."*
> *oscula non aliter numerat iucunda Secundus,*
>   *alter qui calamo paene Catullus erat.*
> *longe sed cumulum superasti, Iane, Catulli:*
>   *parui ter centum, milia terna putans,*
> *centum tu centena dares, millenaque centum –*
>   *felix, ah!, toties pulchra Neaera fuit! –*
> *miliaque imprimeres millena, tot oscula quot sunt*
>   *seu pelago guttae, sidera siue polo.*
> *tertius ipse in idem uolui certamen inire,*
>   *illos si possem uincere forte duos.*
> *ast ego cum sescenta tibi cantare pararem*
>   *basia, sescentis nexa, Camilla, modis,*
> *"Esne mathematicus" dixisti "an miles Amoris?*
>   *suauia dum numeras, suauia ferre nequis!*
> *ter centum ualeant, ualeant haec milia terna!*
>   *da mihi suauiolum – non ego plura rogo –*
> *mellitum, rorans, tenerum, sine fine, uenustum:*
>   *unum tale, inquam, quale neque ante tuli."*

Iunxi labra labris. superum per numina iuro,
suauius hoc solum mille, Catulle, tuis.

Metre: Elegiacs

Translation: *Counting Kisses*

How many sweet kisses mad poets demand! They count out countless kisses: after that, they ask for more! You, learned Catullus, ask for a thousand kisses, then a hundred, then another thousand, then a hundred—you're not done yet—then you add another thousand and another hundred. Who can compute the total? Alas! I need a calculator. The grand total is three thousand, three hundred. Are these enough and more than enough for him? He says no: "As many as are the sands on the shore of Lybia, as many as are the stars, so many will be enough and more than enough for me." In the same way Secundus, who was almost a second Catullus with his pen, counts up delightful kisses. But you far outdid Catullus' pile of kisses, Janus. Thinking little of three thousand, three hundred, you would give ten thousand, and a hundred thousand— ah, so many times fortunate was lovely Neaera!—and you would give a million kisses, as many as are the drops in the sea or the stars in heaven. I wanted to be the third to enter into this contest, to see if I could perhaps surpass those other two. But as I was getting ready, Camilla, to sing myriad kisses to you, applied in myriad ways, "Are you a mathematician," you said, "or a soldier of love? When you count kisses, you can't give kisses! Away with these three hundred, away with these three thousand! Give me a little kiss—I ask for no more—one sweet as honey, dripping with dew, soft, endless, lovely: one kiss, I mean, like I've never had before." I joined my lips with hers. By the gods in heaven, I swear, this single kiss, Catullus, was sweeter than a thousand of yours.

*   *   *

David Money

David Money teaches Neo-Latin literature at the University of Cambridge, for the Faculty of Modern and Medieval Languages, and is a fellow of the *Academia Latinitati Fovendae*; he has published widely on Neo-Latin topics, especially on British verse of the 16th to 18th centuries. As well as trying to be active as a Latin poet, he is interested in encouraging others to develop their talents in this direction, with initiatives such as the 'Inter Versiculos' summer workshop (University of Michigan, 2011).

Ad Ambulatorem Vates Hortantem

David writes: This was composed on 5 May 2010, in honour of *Vates* and its editor, Mark Walker. It plays with the various possibilities of the iambic metre, including its potential variations and ability to include words which cannot fit in dactylic hexameters or elegiacs (anything with one light between two heavy syllables, such as 'ambulator'). The aim is to be playful, and hopefully to suggest that metrical experiments can be quite fun, while encouraging participants in *Vates* towards a spirit of adventure, in whatever direction they may wish to travel. Light verse, then: not to be taken too seriously, but perhaps making some points as it trips along about the inspirational benefits of looking at other new verse, and the need for some kind of control, by both poet and editor. My apologies for the number of technical terms in these comments, for those who may not yet know them all: there is nothing frightening about them once one gets used to them. They are mostly just ways of describing alternative arrangements of heavy and light syllables: the small effort involved in getting to know the terminology of a slightly more 'exotic' metre can be quite worthwhile.

I treat the verse form like the trimeters of Greek tragedy: six feet (or three units of two feet each); the most common variant is a spondee instead of an iamb in the first, third, or fifth foot. I observe a *caesura* (as one must) in the third or fourth foot, and also Porson's law of the final cretic (no *caesura* in the fifth foot, if it is a spondee). The poem starts and ends with 'pure' iambics (lines 1, 2, 16), allowing no variants; then the normal variant, the spondee, appears (lines 3 to 8). Line 9 starts with a dactyl: less common, but fairly tame. Then the pace becomes frantic, allowing frequent anapaests (light-light-heavy) and tribrachs (three light syllables) in lines 10 to 14. Line 12 uses the word for 'tribrach', with a Greek nominative '-ys' ending. Line 13 is particularly wild, running as 'dactyl, tribrach, dactyl, iamb, anapaest, iamb' (note that I treat *temere* as three light syllables, *pace* Lewis and Short). The effect is deliberately jumpy, far from the steady walking pace signalled by more regular iambics. This concentration of variant feet, all allowable in themselves, is not something I would normally recommend: but I enjoyed trying to push the metre towards its limits. The poem winds down at the end from this bout of metrical enthusiasm: line 15 has steadying spondees in all three permitted places, and the final line at last returns to the initial wariness of all these risky variants. Have we completed the walk without tripping up? Let Walker and his readers be the judges of that.

> quis Ambulator audet excitare uim
> poeticam? quis urget, ardet, aut auet?
> aut quis perenne carminis pignus noui

creare gressu gestit incedens suo?
fortasse uates quisque grata peruicax   5
incepta sumat ex recentioribus
diuersioribusque uatibus, legat
libenter omnes excitatorum sales,
denique resurgens aemulo uadat pede.
rapidis pedibus et uaria tractet artium   10
insolita currens loca et amore anapaestico
titubet, tribrachys aut si per aruorum uias
se temere tener insinuet, accipiatur in
gremium poetae. perge, nam passum tuum
laudo; ruentes more qui puro reget,   15
placebit ambulator omnibus uigil.

Metre: Iambic trimeters

Translation:

'To Walker, who encourages poets': Who is this Walker who dares to rouse the force of poetry? Who urges, burns, or desires? Or who longs to create an eternal memorial of new song, going on at his own pace? Perhaps each persistent poet may take welcome ideas from more recent and more diverse poets, and may gladly read all the wit of those who have been roused, and may finally rise up and walk forward with rivalry in his step. He may deal with varied and unusual backwaters of the arts, running with rapid feet; and he may stagger with love of anapaests; or if a tender tribrach rashly inserts itself among the country roads, may it be accepted into the bosom of the poet. Proceed, for I praise your pace. A watchful walker will please all, if he will rule in a pure manner those who rush onwards.

*   *   *

Officium Vatis

(circa una hora compositum, 24.00 – 01.00, 10/11 Jul. 2002)

David writes: This poem has been published in Latin before, but not translated or commented upon. Although I hope the majority of the piece is not too hard to follow, I see, as I translate it, that in parts it lives up to its own prediction that things obvious to a writer as he writes may not be so clear to a reader (even to the writer himself, returning to it later). Nevertheless I do think I see what I meant, and still agree with it, as far as it goes. It is, naturally, on the brief side for an *Ars Poetica*. The aim is to encourage people to get on with it, to write something lively and original without taking themselves too seriously, and to communicate it to others. These simple precepts might, I hope, be in tune with the ethos of *Vates*.

The poem urges us to embrace novelty and humour, including the sort of elephantine metrical playfulness it demonstrates with the fifth-foot spondee *evitandus*. (Our standards for 'humour' need not be too high: if it makes the author smile to think of it, that's a start.) Any genre or approach to composition may work well, though original writing can offer a freshness that tends to be less evident in the traditional exercise of translation from English. Poets who do see themselves as poets (however modest their ambitions) and are true to themselves, may end up pleasing other people as they satisfy their own urge. Among other things, I would like to see more genuine love poetry in contemporary Latin, though some ambiguity and license may be inevitable, as the final lines indicate.

The original circumstances of composition dictated the poem's length, and sense of urgency. I wanted to see how much could reasonably be done in an hour, without sacrificing all sense, at the end of a day's fairly busy composition (100 lines or so) in preparation for flying out to Poland for a Latin poets' workshop and small conference, organised by Anna Elissa Radke: the results of our collective efforts may be found in the volume she entitled *Alaudae* (Hildesheim: Olms, 2005; vol. 5 in the 'Noctes Neolatinae' series; 'Officium Vatis', p. 130). Needless to say, this was not a normal day's work (a normal day's production is zero), but under the stimulation of an imminent self-imposed deadline (self-imposed, because I needn't have taken such new stuff, and could even have tried starting earlier). It really did take about an hour to do this, just after midnight on 10-11 July 2002, and I don't think it was altered thereafter. I say this not (or not entirely) to boast of its facility, or excuse its limitations, but to argue that speedy composition, popular in the Renaissance, can still have a place in modern Latin.

To those starting off on this absorbing intellectual pastime, who may find it a challenge to achieve workable lines quickly, it will hopefully be more encouraging than off-putting to see that 19 LPH (lines per hour) is achievable, though I would more often potter along at a steadier 5 or 10 LPH – much slower if one meets a jam. The secret of minimising jams, I find, is to develop a sense of what will and won't fit where in a line, and to avoid trying anything that will produce awkward gaps to fill; if in doubt, keep it simple, putting the verb, subject and object in their most natural places (metrically), and then fill the gaps. Think first about the parts that will be hardest, usually the line-ends. Check the start and end of each word carefully against its neighbour, watching out for elisions and correct application of the two-consonant rule. It's all too easy to make errors of scansion or grammar: I often do, usually something I neglected to check because I thought I knew it. Never mind; with practice comes the ability to spot many errors for oneself, and it is one of the kindly functions of an editor to save some of the rest from entertaining the smugness of posterity. Be bold, and be a *uates* ...

officium uatis quid sit? si forte Latinas
audeat ad Musas hodierna uoce uenire,
audax sit. cur non? famam sperare furorem
indicat; at placeat primo sibi – nemine laudem
praestante aut meritam aut aliter, priuata parentur
gaudia: se pellat scribendi pura cupido.
ast aliis cupiat monstrare cupidine natum
carmen. ad hunc finem facile – aut non ardua – semper
percipienda canat: quod clare percipit auctor,
sensibus haud hominum diuersis omne uidetur.
carmina si uis redde noua uernacula ueste:
Musa tamen proprias mauult res. apta creare
adfectes linguae. numeros ui strenuus urge –
parce sed ipse tuis nugis sollemniter uti.

cui loqueris? tantum tibi – nec iocus euitandus.
quanquam mentitur non numquam quisque poeta,
ueros exponat (quantum licet) aequus amores
(nomine mutato, si sic sit tutius): ergo
per noctes ualeat longum tolerare laborem.

Metre: Hexameters

Translation: 'The poet's duty'

What might the poet's duty be? If by chance he dares to approach the Latin Muses in today's voice, let him be bold. Why not? To hope for fame is an indication of poetic frenzy. But let him first please himself – if no one proffers praise (whether deserved or otherwise), let private joys be prepared; let the pure desire of writing push itself on. Yet he should desire to show to others the song born from his desire. To this end let him always sing things which are easily understood (or at least not hard); something which the author himself sees clearly is not necessarily quite obvious to people's differing senses. If you like, dress up vernacular songs in some new clothes: but the Muse nevertheless prefers her own fresh material. You should strive to create things fitted to the language. Push on your rhythms forcefully – but don't take your own stuff *too* seriously. Who are you talking to anyway? Just to yourself – nor should a chance for joking be neglected. Although each poet lies often enough, let him fairly lay down his true loves (as much as he can get away with; under a pseudonym, if that's the safer course?); and thus may he have the strength to endure long nocturnal labours.

*   *   *

Nurses – an epigram

A Brief Dissertation on Muses:

(*Muse*: Emma; *Vates*: David Money)

David writes: We are used to Muses as fictional sources of inspiration: Melpomene and her crowd are unlikely to mean much to contemporary poets, however 'real' they may or may not have seemed to Horace. That is why, when there is a real Muse involved, I feel she deserves equal billing with the 'Vates' – especially when she and her colleagues have other valuable skills, such as the ability to poke various devilish devices in one's arm, with the minimum of bloodshed and unpleasantness, and the maximum of good humour.

This epigram, then, was composed on a topic suggested by Emma, during the poet's temporary residence (7-13 August 2012) in Addenbrookes' hospital, Cambridge, ward C4, bed 19; a stay enhanced by a 'room with a view', agreeable room-mates (for which many thanks to Vinod, bed 17, and Steve, bed 18), excellent room-service, and free catering that can match many colleges (at least at lunch-time; dinners perhaps slightly below some high-table standards). Should readers be unfortunate enough to take a tumble in the Cambridge area, I can thoroughly recommend the nursing: and while Latin may not be the first language in use (while English is widely understood, perhaps try out your Polish, Italian, Slovakian, Tagalog, Glaswegian), as you can see, there are Muses available for the Latin poet who asks nicely.

Funnily enough, the issue of 'modern' Muses had previously arisen, during my Latin lectures on verse-composition at Terence Tunberg's 'conventiculum', 2010 and 2011. We settled, I recall, on 'Brenda' of Kentucky, a name chosen by the learned Scottius to represent modern America. And by coincidence – Romans might have called it fate – a real woman named Brenda was indeed inspirational (though not for this particular epigram) during my recent vacation in ward C4. Similarly, visitors to our American verse-writing website, 'Inter Versiculos', may encounter Mildred, our invented rustic Muse of Michigan (and any real Mildreds are invited to step forward with their ideas).

The epigram intends, naturally, to praise nurses; and perhaps slightly to tweak the tail of the more humourless kind of doctor. This should not be taken as any criticism of actual physicians I encountered: whose response to any emergency appeared superb, although it also seemed impossible to find one for non-emergency purposes at the weekend (presumably on the golf-course: a convenience less easily available to the nurses, health-care assistants and so on, who are obliged to work unsocial hours, and deserve our deep thanks for doing so). The epigram contrasts the archetypal nurse, Florence Nightingale, the 'lady with the lamp' of the Crimean war, with another character nicknamed 'bringer of light', the anti-hero of Milton's *Paradise Lost* (the literal meaning of 'Lucifer' is 'bringer of light' – obviously pejorative in the case of Satan, but not generally so in other Latin contexts). *Lucifera*, the feminine form, here elides into the following vowel, so sounding almost identical.

> *Lucifera ad stellas bello tua munera tollit;*
> *Lucifer e stellis doctior arte ruit.*

Metre: Elegiac couplet

Translation:

> She bore a lamp, in wartime, raising up
>   Her task, and most who take it, to the stars;
> Learned 'light-bringer', doctored, over-proud:
>   He sped the other way, from stars to hell.

*   *   *

O Mensa

Iambics addressed politely 'To a Table'

David writes: This poem was one of several composed at Lexington, Kentucky, in 2010: the inspiration for this reflection on the vocative of *mensa* is the oft-repeated story (most recently seen in a film commemorating the late, distinguished Danish linguist, Hans Ørberg, who pioneered the teaching of Latin as a living language, which was shown at the Accademia Vivarium Novum, Rome, 2010) of the young Winston Churchill's puzzlement at the vocative case (Churchill, *My Early Life*). The boy asks his teacher what *o mensa*, in the grammar book, means; the teacher answers, "'o table', used when addressing a table", to which the boy replies, "but I never *do* address a table". I thought the table, to whom no one ever does seem to say anything, might be feeling a little sorry for itself, so I composed this to cheer it up ...

o mensa: plana, comis, utilis comes,
modesta uirgo: rarius quisquam uocat
te uoce clara; rusticos passim pudet
uidere mores, nec politioribus
circumdari (mi mensa) collegis domi.
misella mensa, maesta ne fias, locum
honoris amplum praebeo domestici.
nam crura laudo semper aequali modo
bene ordinata: sic et exemplum potes
monstrare nobis, mensa docta, commodum.
si corda uiolens nostra tempestas quatit,
uiuenda uita semper est aequaliter.

Metre: Iambic trimeter.

Translation: O table, level, kind, useful companion, o modest female: rarely does anyone address you openly; I'm ashamed to see such poor manners, and that you are not, my dear table, surrounded by politer colleagues at home. Poor little table, don't be sad: I offer you an ample place of domestic honour. For I praise your legs, always well-ordered, in an equal manner – and thus you are able to show us a worthwhile example, o learned table: if a violent storm shakes our hearts, life must always be lived levelly.

*   *   *

Verses for Rowley

Celebrating an octogenarian

David writes: The poem below was composed in October 2013, to celebrate the eightieth birthday of someone called Margaret Rowley, whom in fact I have never met – but who sounds well worthy of such a tribute. It is based on various pieces of information about the addressee's life and interests provided by Melanie Soden, the relative who 'commissioned' the poem (if that is the right word), through a mutual friend, Fiona Hook. She asked for something in Latin: it seemed to me that a poem would be better than a little piece of prose rhetoric. Apparently the results went down well enough with the recipient, and her family and friends.

I present it here for a wider readership in almost the same form as the original composition; I omit one couplet, quite personal to the addressee, which she would prefer to keep for her private amusement. Some interesting challenges arose; I aimed to fit her past and present academic interests into the opening couplet – training as a physicist in Oxford, and then a Classics degree in retirement. Taking two disparate adjectives (*physicis, piis*) with the same noun (*artibus*) was my attempt to compress this information. Current recreations follow: cycling in the second couplet, line-dancing in the fifth, chess in the sixth. I thought it important, as she was a former Yorkshire chess champion, to get in the chess; and I quite like the idea of the little wars of wooden monarchs, as well

101

as the chance to allude to Vida's great Renaissance poem on the subject. A large and lively family – seven children, cats that are always having kittens – demanded mention; the garden found a place, but stories about a goat and chickens I didn't find room for.

As a Latin poet, I found it quite stimulating to be writing about someone I *didn't* know, trying to select and use to good effect appropriate ideas from the information that had been provided. It certainly makes a change from addressing personal poems to people I do know, as I have done over the years, along with quite a few other writers of modern Latin. The question arises, with such 'occasional' poetry, of whether its interest can extend beyond the original 'occasion' for its production. I hope it often can. But it needs to make some effort to arrest the attention of those later readers for whom the original persons and occasion have no particular significance. In the history of our art-form, the genre has a large, if sometimes problematic, place: something I have tried to explore further in my chapter on 'Epigrams and Occasional Poetry' in the forthcoming *Oxford Handbook of Neo-Latin*, edited by Sarah Knight and Stefan Tilg.

In past centuries, a lot of occasional poetry celebrated monarchs and other dignitaries. In our (sometimes) more democratic age, it is nice to see the individual qualities of more 'ordinary' people celebrated. As far as I am concerned, future commissions are welcome (those interested may contact me on dkm14@cam.ac.uk); other poets who contribute to *Vates* might indeed feel similarly, and be willing to put their services, in suitable circumstances and perhaps for an appropriate small reward, at the disposal of those by whom a new Latin poem might be appreciated – why not ask them, if the prospect of eternal fame intrigues you?

A Latin Tribute to Margaret Rowley
On her Eightieth Birthday

> nouisti physicis dudum primordia rerum
> artibus, et senior pristina prata piis.
> lustro iam decimo sexto es robusta peracto,
> pergis enim binis adueherisque rotis.
> sunt quas tam grauiter premit octogesimus annus,
> quas tardat tempus deminuitque dies:
> qualiter haud uitam stolide tractare uideris,
> indomito sequeris laeta uigore uiam.
> linea saltantes leuiter disponit amicos,
> hortum florenti sedula mente colis.
> delectatque diu bene notus Scacchia ludus,
> lignosi regis ludicra bella iuuant.
> felibus et mulcens fecundis cincta sedebis;
> uiuas septena prole beata tua.
> illustri uigeas octogenaria laude:
> gaudeat omnis homo, floreat omne genus.

Metre: Elegiacs

Translation:

Long ago you learnt the origin of things with a physicist's arts, and more recently you explored ancient fields with devoted skill. Now you are still robust, having passed your sixteenth *lustrum* [a five-year period, sometimes used by the Romans to mark ages; e.g. Horace *Odes* 4.1.6], for you proceed and are carried forward on two wheels. There are ladies whose eighty years weigh them down, whom time slows, and each day diminishes: you do not seem to be like them, dully stretching out life – instead, you happily follow your own path with undefeated vigour. A line keeps your lightly-dancing friends in order; you carefully cultivate your garden with a flourishing mind. The game of chess, which you know well, has long delighted you [cf. Marco Girolamo Vida's poem, *Scacchia Ludus*]: the wooden king's laughable wars give pleasure. And you will sit, stroking, surrounded by fecund cats; may you live happy in your seven-fold offspring. May you thrive as an octogenarian, much-praised; may everyone rejoice, may your whole family flourish.

*   *   *

Marc Moskowitz

Marc Moskowitz is a Latin poet, and the curator of the very neglected site Contemporary Latin Poetry (www.suberic.net/~marc/latinpoetry.html). By day he writes code for online publishing web sites.

Fabula Vulpina

Marc writes: This poem was written as a response to some recent (as of 2010) political happenings in the USA.

> *fabula quam recitas, uulpecula, prouocat ignem.*
> *osa es tu quercum, quercus nunc ecce perusta.*
> *forte sed esuries, quondam, sine quoque patrono;*
> *frustra per siluam quaeres uestigia glandis.*

Metre: Hexameters

Translation:

> The story you tell, little fox, incites a fire. You hated the oak, so now behold the oak in ashes. But perhaps you will hunger, someday, without all your patrons; in vain you will search through the forest for traces of an acorn.

* * *

Paul Murgatroyd

Paul Murgatroyd is a professor in the department of Classics at McMaster University in Canada. He is the author of eleven books and over 90 articles on Greek and especially Latin literature, and is at present working on a translation and critical appreciation of Virgil *Aeneid* 2. He has also published original Latin poetry and translations, a collection of which was issued by the Edwin Mellen Press in 1991 as *Neo-Latin Poetry A Collection of Translations into Latin Verse and Original Compositions.*

Vesica

Paul writes: This epigram was produced under the inspiration of one of my favourite poets: Ovid, specifically *Amores* 1.9.1-2.

> cymbia, uina, calix nostrae sunt dulcia menti,
> tristia uesicae cymbia, uina, calix.

Metre: Elegiac couplet

Translation:

Drinking-cups, wine, wine-cups are delights for our mind, banes for our bladder are drinking-cups, wine, wine-cups.

*   *   *

Satirical Epigrams

Paul writes: These translations from Greek originals in the Palatine Anthology are an attempt to do justice to the Greek epigrammatists.

A.P. 11.68

> Leuconoe, dicunt quidam te tingere crines;
> sed coma nigra tibi nempe coempta foro.

Leuconoe, some say that you dye your hair; but your black hair was doubtless bought by you in the forum.

A.P. 11.186

> cum coruus cantat, pereunt ex omine multi;
> cum Marius cantat, coruus et ipse perit.

When the raven sings, many die in accordance with the omen; when Marius sings, even the raven itself dies.

A.P. 11.224

> *Victorem nudum uidit dixitque Priapus:*
> *'me miserum, magno est numine maior homo.'*

Priapus saw Victor naked and said: 'Oh dear, a mortal is bigger than a big divinity.'

A.P. 11.226

> *sit tibi terra leuis, letum cum lumina claudet,*
> *ut facile e terra te catuli rapiant.*

May the earth rest lightly on you, when death closes your eyes, so that the dogs can easily drag you from the earth.

A.P. 11.277

> *in somnis quondam segnissimus Atta cucurrit;*
> *nunc uigilat, rursus currere non cupiens.*

The extremely indolent Atta once ran in a dream; now he stays awake, not wanting to run again.

A.P.11.80

> *marmoreum grate pugiles hic ponimus Apim.*
> *uulnera nam nobis non pugil ille dedit.*

We boxers here are setting up a marble statue of Apis in gratitude. For that boxer did not wound us.

A.P. 11.113

> *quod medicis manibus statuam Iouis attigit Agis,*
> *nunc Iouis et statuae soluimus exsequias.*

Because Agis touched a statue of Jupiter with his doctor's hands, now we are performing funeral rites for Jupiter and the statue.

A.P.11.192

> pendenti pendens iuxta Nasta inuidet Afro
> liuidulus, quod crux celsior illa sua est.

Nasta, crucified nearby, envies crucified Afer, jealous because that man's cross is higher than his own.

A.P. 11.223

> Furnius an futuat ne quaeras. namque ego noui:
> haudquaquam futuit Furnius, os futuit.

Don't ask if Furnius fucks. For I know: Furnius doesn't fuck at all, his mouth fucks.

A.P. 11.236

> nempe mali Cilices cuncti; Cilicum tamen unus
> uir bonus est Cinyras; est Cinyrasque Cilix.

Without doubt all Cilicians are bad; but alone of the Cilicians Cinyras is a good man; and Cinyras is a Cilician.

A.P. 11.315

> tu cubital nuper cernebas, Zoile, Nattae,
> nec iam Natta suum cernere quit cubital.

Zoilus, you recently set eyes on Natta's cushion, and Natta can no longer set eyes on his cushion.

Metre: Elegiacs

*   *   *

First World War Poems

Paul Murgatroyd writes: Since I first read some World War One poets at the age of 15 I have always been very moved by such poetry. A few months ago my sister-in-law gave me for a birthday present a selection that contained several pieces which I had not seen before, and which I immediately wanted to translate into Latin.

(1)

> nostra hic ossa iacent quando non uiuere dulce

nobis et patriam sic maculare fuit.
non uitae iactura grauis; iuuenes tamen illam
   esse grauem credunt, et fuimus iuuenes.

Metre: Elegiacs

Translation: *Here Dead We Lie* (A.E. Housman)

> Here dead we lie
> Because we did not choose
> To live and shame the land
> From which we sprung.
>
> Life, to be sure,
> Is nothing much to lose.
> But young men think it is,
> And we were young.

*   *   *

(2)

dic mihi, num refert ambo deperdere crura?
   namque tibi mites semper erunt homines.
uenati redeunt alii dapibusque fruuntur,
   sed potes inuidiam dissimulare tuam.
dic mihi, num refert ambos deperdere ocellos?
   sunt operae caecis scilicet egregiae.
cumque sedens uultum et uertens ad lumen in horto
   res repetes, mites semper erunt homines.
dic mihi, num refert per somnum inferna uidere?
   nempe mero laetus nec memor esse potes.
nec, gnari te pro patria pugnasse, uocabunt
   te uecordem homines, solliciti nec erunt.

Metre: Elegiacs

Translation: *Does It Matter?* (Siegfried Sassoon)

> Does it matter? - losing your legs?...
> For people will always be kind,
> And you need not show that you mind
> When the others come in after hunting
> To gobble their muffins and eggs.
>
> Does it matter? - losing your sight?...
> There's such splendid work for the blind;
> And people will always be kind,
> As you sit on the terrace remembering
> And turning your face to the light.
>
> Do they matter? - those dreams from the pit?...
> You can drink and forget and be glad,

And people won't say that you're mad;
For they'll know that you've fought for your country
And no one will worry a bit.

*   *   *

(3)

perdidit hic uitam, hic membrum; sed perdidit ille,

di, mentem caram: praemia quanta feret?

hic fruitur laudes, hic pacem; garrit at ille,

demisso mento: dic mihi, quid fruitur?

naufragium belli est; illi et mens turbida torpet;

tanto pro damno praemia quanta feret?

Metre: Elegiacs

Translations: *What Reward?* (Winifred M. Letts)

You gave your life, boy,
And you gave a limb:
But he who gave his precious wits,
Say, what reward for him?

One has his glory,
One has found his rest.
But what of this poor babbler here
With chin sunk on his breast?

Flotsam of battle,
With brain bemused and dim,
O god, for such a sacrifice,
Say, what reward for him?

*   *   *

(4)

non fodisse ualens, non audens despoliare,

ut caperem uulgus, falsa locutus ego.
omnia quae dixi constat nunc falsa fuisse,

inque illos cogor quos ego perdideram.
decepti per me certe feruentque dolentque:

tot quid praetexens conciliem iuuenes?

Metre: Elegiacs

Translation: *A Dead Statesman* (Rudyard Kipling)

I could not dig: I dared not rob:
Therefore I lied to please the mob.
Now all my lies are proved untrue

And I must face the men I slew.
What tale shall serve me here among
Mine angry and defrauded young?

*   *   *

(5)

in uitam ueni, remeans ex urbe timoris,
ex ferruginea et fracta tellure doloris.
cum nauem caeli subter labentia signa
iactaret pontus, clamaret uentus in armis,
frigidus horrebam; sed carmina, uina, calorem
uersabam mecum, fruiturus talia rursus
per paucos paruosque dies. sum uectus et inde
dormitans raeda, Romamque repente propinquam
uersabam mecum. "Romae nunc nempe puellam
(ut prius) inueniam, facilem uanamque puellam,"
aiebam tacitus, "cuius digitos retinebo;
osque genasque meis contingam deinde labellis;
osque genasque obliuiscar post tempore paruo.
illa obliuiscar certe, cum rursus adibo
tellurem ad ferrugineam fractamque doloris,
res udas, foedas, atque anxia taedia belli."

Metre: Hexameters

Translation: *On Leave* (Gilbert Frankau)

I came from the City of Fear,
From the scarred brown land of pain,
Back into life again...
And I thought, as the leave-boat rolled
Under the veering stars -
Wind a-shriek in her spars -
Shivering there, and cold,
Of music, of warmth, and of wine -
To be mine
For a whole short week...
And I thought, adrowse in the train,
Of London, suddenly near;
And of how - small doubt - I should find
There, as of old,
Some woman - foolishly kind:
Fingers to hold,
A cheek,
A mouth to kiss - and forget,
Forget in a little while,
Forget
When I came again
To the scarred brown land of pain,
To the sodden things and the vile,

And the tedious battle-fret.

*   *   *

Uxor Tiresiae

Paul writes: I got the inspiration for this from Carol Anne Duffy's poem *From Mrs Tiresias*, and I felt that as a Classicist I could take the basic idea further in terms of wit, allusion and inventiveness (along the general lines of Ovid's *Heroides*).

haec ego nostro scripta uiro sapientia mitto,
    uir si noster adhuc ese potest mulier.
montanas pridem placuit tibi uisere siluas;
    portabas caeci more senis baculum.
o utinam caecus uero lippusue fuisses!
    sed tu serpentes, stulte, coire uides;
nec uidisse satis: baculo disiungere pergis;
    plaga grauis colubris, plaga mihi grauior.
namque refers longasque comas faciemque tenellam
    et maiora meis pectora pectoribus.
Iunonis speciem, Iunonis grandia membra,
    Iunonis nitidos tu superas oculos.
mox rapis armillasque meas strophiumque superbum,
    inficis et fucis ora decora meis.
deinde uetas me labra tuis coniungere labris,
    ne post audires praua puella timens.
teque ardet multus caelebs multusque maritus;
    uxorem fallis, fallis at usque uiris.
ante mihi segnis, peccas per mille figuras,
    nunc noua percipiens gaudia concubitus.
optasti tandem dominis ex omnibus unum,
    illiusque domum denique fida colis.
mutata forma, quis sis non nouit amator;
    quis sit at ille quidem dissimulare nequis.
anne tuum nescis te nunc corrumpere fratrem,
    caecus mente, oculis auriculisque tuis?
mox tu frater eris fratri pariterque marita;
    mox tu mater eris, moxque amita et patruus.
sed si forte tuae capient te taedia uitae,
    mensque erit ad nuptam, nupta, redire tuam,
ne redeas. nam, quod tu diuinare nequibas,
    tristis eram tecum, te sine laetificor.
si redeas uero, me iam donisque petentes

multos inuenias blanditiisque procos.
sed potius remeans uideas colubros coeuntes,
   feminea rursus percutiasque manu;
tum precor e plaga penem testesque receptes;
   denique eas ipsam te futuasque precor.

Metre: Elegiacs

Translation: *His Wife to Tiresias*

I am sending these words of wisdom to my man, if indeed a woman can still be my man. Some time ago you decided to visit the woods on the mountain; you carried a staff like a blind old man. Oh, I wish you had been really blind or blear-eyed! But you saw, you fool, that snakes were copulating, and seeing was not enough: you proceeded to part them with your stick. The blow was grievous for the snakes; the blow was more grievous for me. For you came back with long hair and a soft face and breasts bigger than my breasts. You outdid Juno's beauty, Juno's large frame, Juno's sparkling eyes. Soon you stole my bracelets and my splendid bra, and you coloured your pretty face with my cosmetics. Then you forbade me to join my lips to your lips, fearing that subsequently you would be called a depraved girl. Many bachelors and many husbands burned for you; you cheated on your wife, but you always cheated on her with men. Formerly sluggish for me, you committed adultery in a thousand positions, now deriving new pleasure from intercourse. Finally you chose one out of all your boyfriends, and you live in his house, faithful at last. Since your form has been changed, your lover does not know who you are, but you certainly cannot pretend to be ignorant of who he is. Can it really be that you, blind in your mind, eyes and ears, do not know that you are corrupting your own brother? Soon you will be brother to your brother and at the same time wife; soon you will be a mother, soon an aunt too and an uncle. But if you get bored with your life, and have a mind, wife, to return to your wife, don't return. For (something which you were unable to divine) I was unhappy with you, I am delighted without you. But if in fact you were to return, you would find many suitors now courting me with both gifts and endearments. But rather, while coming back home, see copulating snakes and strike them again with your feminine hand; I pray that then you get back your penis and testicles; I pray that finally you go shaft yourself.

*   *   *   **

7 Epigrams from A.P. 7

Paul writes: These translations from Greek originals in the Palatine Anthology are an attempt to do justice to the Greek epigrammatists.

7.33

   'tu, quod eras bibulus, cecidisti.' 'uerum ego uixi.
     non bibis ipse, tamen tu quoque nempe cades.'

7.71

   hic iacet Archilochus. uiolans Helicona cruore,

felle ferox tinxit carmina uipereo.
tu pede praeteriens tacito obmutesce, uiator,
ne uespas moueas quae monumenta colunt.

7.288

me simul eiecto potiuntur terra fretumque:
uiscera nam pisces, ora sed ossa tenet.

7.308

quinque annos uixi, uitaeque dies ego paucos
carpsi, sed uitae sic mala pauca tuli.

7.319

mortuus est Timon. sed adhuc saeuissimus ille.
morsus Timonis, Cerbere, tu caueas.

7.461

omniparens Tellus, subter te nunc iacet Aeson.
ne grauis esto illi: non fuit ille tibi.

7.469

hic iacet Hagniades, homines qui funditus omnes
fama praeteriit praeteriitque malis.

Metre: Elegiacs

Translations:

7.33
'Because you were fond of drink you died.' 'Yes, but I lived life to the full. You don't drink yourself, but you too will certainly die.'

7.71
Here lies Archilochus. Profaning Helicon with blood, he ferociously drenched poetry in viper's gall. Be quiet as you pass by on silent feet, traveller, so you don't rouse the wasps that inhabit his tomb.

7.288
The land and sea together possess me cast ashore: for the fish have my flesh and the beach has my bones.

7.308
I lived for five years, and I enjoyed few days of life, but in this way I endured few of life's evils.

7.319
Timon is dead. But he is still very savage. Cerberus, be on your guard against Timon's bites.

7.461

Earth, mother of all, Aeson now lies beneath you. Don't be heavy on him: he was not [heavy] on you.

7.469

Here lies Hagniades, who completely surpassed all men in fame and surpassed them in misfortunes.

*   *   *

Meditations

Paul writes: These verses take as their starting point various snippets from the *Meditations* of Marcus Aurelius. All are elegiac couplets.

3.10

parua quidem uita est, post mortem famaque parua:
non homines norint te neque se stolidi.

5.17

non adeunda sequi summa est insania certe;
cogunturque mali non adeunda sequi.

2.2

affectus famulus facilis, uacuus rationis,
deplorat praesens, fata futura pauens.

7.21

mente cadent hominesque tua cito cum moriere,
mortuus atque hominum tu cito mente cades.

4.3

per spatium breue fama patet, stat per breue tempus;
sunt plausus, laudes, praemia nempe nihil.
paruulus est orbis, paruusque hic angulus orbis;
hic quanti, quales te celebrant homines?

4.48

uita sunt functi reges qui mente maligna
uitam uix dederant ciuibus ante suis;
mortuus est medicus qui mortes arcuit aegris;
perditus est dux qui perdidit innumeros.
quam fragiles sunt res humanae quamque caducae!
qui modo semen eras, tu cito puluis eris.

Translations:

3.10

Life is certainly a small thing, and fame after death is a small thing: dull human beings won't know of you and won't know themselves either.

5.17

To pursue the unattainable is surely supreme insanity; yes and bad men are under a compulsion to pursue the unattainable.

2.2

The tractable slave of passion, devoid of reason, deplores the present, while fearing his future lot.

7.21

You will soon forget humanity when you die, and when you're dead humanity will soon forget you.

4.3

Fame spreads over a little area, lasts over a little period of time; applause, praise, prizes are assuredly nothing. The world is small, and here is a small corner of the world; here how many, what type of men praise you?

4.48

Finished with life are the kings who in the past reluctantly granted life to their subjects in a grudging spirit; the doctor who fended off death from the sick is dead; the general who destroyed countless men is destroyed. How flimsy and transient are things human! You who were just now semen will soon be dust.

*   *   *

Tria Carmina

Paul writes: The second and third of these three poems need no comment. I got the inspiration for the first from the famous scene in the film *Spartacus* where, after the big battle, Spartacus is demanded by the victorious Romans and before he can identify himself many of his men get up and say "I'm Spartacus" – I've taken that down to his grave(s)!

(1) Ego Sum Spartacus

Spartacus hic situs est, immiti marte peremptus;
   praedator, miles, dux, gladiator erat.

Spartacus hic situs est, immiti marte peremptus;
   praedator, miles, dux, gladiator erat.

115

Spartacus hic situs est, immiti marte peremptus;
praedator, miles, dux, gladiator erat.

*   *   *

(2) Medusa

cum nitido clipeo Perseus incedit et ense,
*   sed grauis horrendam Gorgona somnus habet.*
illius in somnis incedens pulcher amator
*   letiferam faciem conspicit et superest.*

*   *   *

(3) Anus

deflet anus ueneranda legens Nasonis Amores,
*   quae quondam placuit, quaeque Corinna fuit.*

*   *   *

Metre: Elegiacs

Translations:

(1) Here lies Spartacus, killed by cruel war; he was a robber, soldier, a leader, a gladiator etc.

(2) With his bright shield and sword Perseus advances, but a deep sleep holds the dreadful Gorgon. In her dream a handsome lover advancing [=comes to her and] looks at her deadly face and survives.

(3) While she reads Ovid's *Amores*, tears are shed by a venerable old lady, who was once attractive, and who was Corinna.

*   *   *

The Song of the Sirens

Paul writes: Ovid was fond of producing his own version of something in a preceding poet, and would often expand his source. I thought that in the spirit of Ovid I would redo the song of the Sirens at Homer *Odyssey* 12.184ff., trying to make it melodious, stylish and amusing.

huc ades, huc aures aduerte, illustris Ulixe;
*   nam pennata loqui uerba tibi uolumus.*

116

mox coram te Scylla rapax sociosque prehendet
  et mandet lente uiscera, corda, genas;
mox mittet nubemque nigram tibi Iuppiter asper,
  funesto et puppim fulmine percutiet.
hic permanat pax aeterna quiesque profunda:
  tuto nobiscum tu potius remane.
accipe quae Troia Troes tulerint et Achiui
  et tua quid coniunx quid faciatque puer.
Penelope penem diui deserta petebat,
  Panaque Mercurio Penelope peperit;
nunc centum iuuenes per portas illa patentes
  admittit; centum continueque ineunt.
Telemachus puerique puer iam prauus amator
  cum tenero nato Nestoris usque iacet.
quid tibi cum tali puero, cum coniuge tali?
  nunc spernens nuptam dic 'mea uita, uale'.
uiuimus hic solae; nos ambas solus habebis;
  nos ambas uno fas tenuisse toro.
iungimus et uenerem uolucres per mille figuras;
  nequitias nostras uincere nemo potest.
dulce et amare et amore mori. mox tu moriere;
  pallebis, cuncto corpore nullus eris.
carmina nostra audis, an cera clauditur auris?
  quidni nobiscum carmina participes?
ad numeros nostros laeto pede percute terram
  et pulsa palma tympana tenta cita.
segnis inersque fugis pulchras facilesque puellas?
  uiuere non gestis? segnis inersque fugis.

*   *   *

Metre: Elegiacs

Translation:

Come here, turn your ears here, illustrious Ulysses; for we want to speak winged words to you. Soon before your eyes rapacious Scylla will seize your companions and slowly chew their entrails, hearts, eyes; and soon angry Jupiter will send a black cloud to you and strike your ship with a deadly thunderbolt. Here eternal peace and deep repose [of death] are diffused: rather remain safely with us. Hear what the Trojans and Greeks endured at Troy and what your wife and son are doing. When deserted, Penelope sought the penis of a god, and Penelope bore Pan to Mercury; now she takes in a hundred young men through her broad gateway; and a hundred [young men] continually enter. And the boy Telemachus, already the depraved lover of a boy, lies constantly with Nestor's tender son. What do you want with such a boy, with such a wife? Now, rejecting your spouse, say 'Farewell, my darling/life'. We live/survive alone here; you alone will have us both; it is permitted for you to embrace us both in one and the same bed. We couple swiftly/birds in a thousand positions; nobody can outdo our naughtiness/evil. It is sweet to love and to die of love. Soon you will die; you will be pale, and your whole body will have shrunk to nothing. Do you hear our song, or are your ears blocked with wax? Why don't you join in the song with us? In time to our melody pound the ground with happy feet and strike a taut drum with a speedy hand. Are you fleeing beautiful and willing girls, spiritless/impotent and unmanly/impotent? Aren't you keen to enjoy life/live/survive? You are fleeing, spiritless/impotent and unmanly/impotent.

*   *   *

Tithonus & Lotophagi

Paul writes: In both these poems my narrative follows the simultaneous technique found in ancient art, presenting together a few significant moments in the story (with links and contrasts). In the first, the handsome youth Tithonus was loved by Dawn, who won immortality for him, but forgot to ask for eternal youth, so that he lived on but grew very old and decrepit. In the second poem, on his return from Troy Odysseus reached the land of the Lotus-eaters. He sent some men to reconnoitre, and they were offered the flowery lotus fruit, which made them forget all about home. Odysseus dragged them back to their ship in tears and sailed off with them.

(1) Tithonus

> garrit perque solum serpit pulcherrimus infans,
>> quem despectat amans mater amansque pater.
>
> ardet diua decens, iuuenis pulcherrimus ardet,
>> facundas fundit blanditiasque hilaris,
> mox uenerem iungit uehemens et amatus amator
>> suauia diuinae sauia dat dominae.
>
> obsitus aeuo est perque solum iam serpere non quit;
>> despectus garrit, tristis, iners, fragilis.
> foetida cui pellis madidique infantia nasi.
>> tabida membra dolent; mentis inopsque iacet.
> purpureaeque manus et lumina lucida diuae
>> ambriosiaeque comae labraque rara latent.

*   *   *

Metre: Elegiac couplets

Translation:

A very handsome infant, at whom his loving mother and loving father look down, babbles and crawls across the floor. An attractive goddess is

118

in love, and a very handsome young man is in love and joyful(ly) pours out eloquent blandishments, soon he strenuous(ly) makes love and, a beloved lover, gives sweet kisses to his divine mistress. He is smothered by old age, and now cannot crawl across the floor; despised he babbles, sad/repulsive, feeble/incapable of movement/with no spirit, frail/brittle. To whom [there is] a stinking hide and the childishness of a wet nose; his emaciated limbs ache; he lies there, devoid of wits. The goddess' rosy hands and bright eyes and ambrosial hair and exquisite lips are unnoticed [by him].

*   *   *

(2) Lotophagi

insolita in miro scintillant sidera caelo,
    dum uenti languent, lunaque solque nitent.
undis tunduntur lapidosaque litora mutis;
    e tenerisque rosis rorat amoenus amor.
usque inter lustra amnis iners pergitque reditque,
    usque sub arboribus frigus et umbra iuuant.
lotos luxuriat dulcis per pinguia rura,
    Lotophagis laetis pomaque odora placent.
otia lotos alit, suauissima somnia gignens;
    incantans animos, otia lotos alit.

Lotophagi Danais donant errantibus almi
    mellitos fructus floridulosque cibos.
dux uulgari mente tamen mox detrahit illos
    deliciis raris ambrosiaque plaga,
ad porcos rediens catulos et pulice plenos,
    stercoris ad cumulos congeriesque fimi.
illi flent. fletus nunc primum funditur illic
    et multo maculat gramina multa sale.

de salsis lotos lacrimis perit herbaque cuncta,
    iam miseri pereunt Lotophagique fame.
omnia sunt deserta, situ senta, exanimata.
    pullo sub caelo saepe sonant gemitus.

Metre: Elegiac couplets

Translation:

In an amazing sky unfamiliar stars glitter, while the winds languish, and the moon and sun shine. The pebbly shore is pounded by silent waves, and charming love is distilled from tender roses. Constantly amid the woodland a sluggish stream moves onward and flows backward, constantly beneath the trees the cool and shade give delight. The sweet lotus flourishes throughout the fertile countryside, and its fragrant fruit pleases the happy Lotus-eaters. The lotus nurtures leisure/relaxation, producing very pleasant dreams; enchanting minds, the lotus nurtures leisure/relaxation. The kindly Lotus-eaters give wandering Greeks their honey-sweet fruit, their flowery food. But the leader, endowed with an ordinary/common mind, soon drags them from the exquisite delights and ambrosial region, returning to pigs and dogs full of fleas, to heaps of manure and piles of excrement. They weep. Tears are now shed there for the first time, and spoil lots of plants with lots of salt. As a result of the salty tears the lotus and all the vegetation is perishing, and now the poor Lotus-eaters are perishing of hunger. Everything is deserted, rough with decay, dead. Beneath a sombre sky groans often ring out.

*   *   *

Carthaginis Occasus

Paul writes: Following the Editor's suggestion about rhythmic trochaic verse in *Vates* #9 I found that I could get some powerful effects. I have produced an impressionistic sketch of the fall of Carthage, which could be viewed as a pendant to Marco Cristini's *Romae Occasus*, also in *Vates* #9.

dies mortis, dies atra
delet alta munimenta,
frangens ossa, calcans ora.

quantus est tectorum fragor,
quantus territorum tremor,
quantus miserorum clamor!

milites Romani vates
doctos caedunt et cantores
et sculptores et pictores;

Phoebi statuamque prendunt
auream at aurum scindunt
summum opus et exstinguunt.

arae sacrae sunt foedatae,
ruptae sunt aularum ualuae,
stratae rarae sunt columnae.

pereunt iam ipsa busta
ueneranda et uestusta,
ignibus sed nigris usta.

uiolatae sunt matronae,
temeratae sunt puellae,
uetulae sunt uitiatae.

Hasdrubalis coniunx caedit
inque ignem natos iacit,
inque ignem ipsa salit.

capientes saeuas dapes,
dominos consumunt canes,
morientes mordent aues;

dentes dilacerant fibras,
ora ebibunt medullas,
rostra perforant pupillas.

dux Romanus minus gaudet.
hic dum fatum Troiae maeret,
cladem talem Romae timet.

obtruncata mater iacet,
propter illam pater tabet,
inter illos infans deflet.

urbs superba humo fumat,
nihil stat ac nihil restat,
trux hyaena hic cacchinnat.

Metre: Rythmic Trochaic

Translation: The day of death, the dark day, destroys lofty fortifications, breaking bones, trampling faces.

How great is the crashing of buildings, how great is the trembling of the terrified, how great is the shouting of the wretched!

Roman soldiers slaughter expert poets and singers and sculptors and painters;

and they seize the golden statue of Apollo and hack apart the gold and obliterate a supreme work of art.

Sacred altars are polluted, mansions' doors are broken through, exquisite pillars are strewn on the ground.

Now the very tombs perish, venerable and ancient, but burnt by black fires.

Matrons are violated, girls are sexually assaulted, old women are raped.

Hasdrubal's wife kills their children and throws them into the fire and leaps into the fire herself.

Eating savage feasts, dogs devour their owners, birds bite the dying;

teeth tear entrails to pieces, mouths swallow marrow, beaks bore through pupils.

The Roman general does not rejoice. While he mourns for the fate of Troy, he fears a similar disaster for Rome.

A mother lies beheaded, near her a father is rotting, between them an infant is crying.

A proud city smokes from the ground, nothing stands and nothing survives, here a fierce hyena laughs.

*   *   *

Epitaphs

Paul writes: These are all genuine epitaphs. I took them from G. Grigson *The Faber Book of Epigrams and Epitaphs*, W.H. Beable *Epitaphs Graveyard Humour and Eulogy*, and W.H. Howe *Here Lies*. The metre is Elegiac couplets.

(1)

> hic iacet uxor nostra, recens quae fata subivit;
> risus nemo edit, nemo ciet lacrimas.
> coniugis umbra meae quid agat, quas venerit oras,
> non ullus nunc scit, scire nec ullus avet.

My wife is dead, and here she lies,
Nobody laughs and nobody cries:
Where she is gone to and how she fares,
Nobody knows, and nobody cares.

(2)

> bustum hoc vincent nulla dehinc monumenta, viator.
> hic iacet Augustus: respice, siste, caca.

Posterity will ne'er survey
A nobler grave than this:
Here lie the bones of Castlereagh:
Stop, traveller, and piss.

(3)

> certe nos cuncti morti debemur acerbae.
> fugit vita mihi; iam tibi vita fugit.

We must all die, there is no doubt;
Your glass is running, mine is out.

(4)

in tumulo mortem video nunc vincere vitam:
  una cum geminis coniugibus iaceo.

Death here advantage hath of life I spye
One husband with two wives at once may lye.
                    (Thos. Alleyn and his two wives, 1650)

(5)

lumina aperta mihi; prospexi lumine cauto;
  prospectus piguit; mox mihi carpta quies.

Oped my eyes, took a peep;
Didn't like it, went to sleep.
                    (of a baby one month old)

(6)

qui legis hoc, epulas ego multas usque peredi;
  sed me nunc multi vermiculi peredunt.

Gentle Reader, Gentle Reader,
  Look on the spot where I do lie.
I was always a very good feeder,
  But now the worms do feed on I.

(7)

pauper ego vixi, pauper vitamque reliqui.
  pauper erat funus; nullus erat gemitus.

Poorly lived
And poorly died
Poorly buried
And no one cried.

(8)

ingenio fuit illa bono, nec mente maligna;
  docta fuitque loqui, nec fuit illa loquax.

Her manners mild, her temper such!
Her language good, and not too much.

(9)

huic nitor (ut queritur lunae de luce viator)
  nempe venustus erat, nempe nimisque brevis.

123

She had no fault save what travellers give the moon:
Her light was lovely, but she died too soon.

(10)

    ille obiit. paulum conata est illa sine illo
      vivere nec potuit. protinus illa obiit.

He first deceased; she for a little tried
To live without him, liked it not, and died.

(11)

    hac frutices tellure sero, carissima coniunx:
      sic isto tumulo vivet adhuc aliquid.
    o bene quod quondam frutices, quibus est pereundum,
      ad vitam redeunt, tu tamen haud redies.

I plant these shrubs upon your grave, dear wife,
That something on this spot may boast of life.
Shrubs must wither and all earth must rot;
Shrubs may revive: but you, thank heaven, will not.

*   *   *

Herimannus Nouocomensis

Herimannus Nouocomensis was the Latin nickname of Ermanno Pizzotti, an Italian lover of Latin and Greek who lived in Como; he held a degree in chemistry and worked in a public chemical laboratory in Italy. He took part in the *Colloquia* held by the Finnish Public Radio YLE for some years, then started to cooperate with *Ephemeris*, a magazine entirely written in Latin founded in Warsaw. Ermanno passed away in April 2015.

Duo Carmina Ad Dies Natales Amici et Amicae Celebrandos

Herimannus writes: These two short poems are really private. They are dedicated to two friends of mine, with whom I spent the most beautiful years of my life in Ferrara, where I attended the Liceo Ludovico Ariosto in the '70s and built up my knowledge of classical languages. In the first poem *Die natali Andreae* you will find a topographic reference to the monastery next to the small church of Santa Monica, where my classroom was located in my first two school years: in those times too many young people aspired to take classical studies and the building was not large enough. Also other dear schoolfellows and friends are named. I tried to recall the mood of familiarity and mutual trust in the wonderful scene of the Estensi's town.

The second poem *Die natali Isabellae* pays honour to my dearest friend, whose height reminded me of a poplar: these trees are the usual background of that part of the Po River Basin and in an ancient myth are Phaeton's sisters mourning on the river banks. But her physical beauty moved my soul only a bit: I did not fall in love, and that is why our friendship is so lasting. The only persons who have read these verses until now are the dedicatees.

(1) Die natali Andreae

> quot decurrerunt hiemes et lucida uera,
> > Andrea, ab autumno quo puerum ad Monicae
> diuinae templum me contulit Aeneadarum
> > in ueterem sermonem immoderatus amor!
> tunc te cognoui, grati tunc inuicem eramus,
> > ortaque mox dulcis mutua amicitia:
> quam ualde augebant permulta uerba iocosa
> > doctrinae studia et seria colloquia.
> o quotiens mater mea uel tua Fabriciiue
> > siue Petri Marci dulcia amica tulit!
> o quotiens rapide tota est Ferraria diua
> > lustrata a nobis uere hieme in nebula!
> quae tempus rapuit: nouum et ignotum incipit aeuum,
> > nec iuuenes quae nos maluimus legerent.

atqui durat adhuc lapillus amicitiae tot
post annos, aeque splendidus atque adamas.

Nouocomi, V die ante Nonas Octobres MMIII

Metre: Elegiacs

Translation: *On Andrea's Birthday*

> How many winters, how many sunny springs have passed, since the autumn when my immoderate love for the old speech of Aeneas' descendants moved me, a boy, to the church of Saint Monica! Then I knew you, we used to be in a good relationship and soon a nice mutual friendship began: this was considerably increased with facetious jokes, school studies and grave conversations. How many times my mother or yours or Fabrice's or Peter Mark's brought us flavoured sweets! How many times we scoured divine Ferrara speedily in spring, in winter, in the fog! Time took away all this: now a new unknown age is beginning, and young people would not like to read what we used to love. Nevertheless the small stone of our friendship is still lasting after so many years, as bright as a diamond. Como, October 3rd 2003

*   *   *

(2) Die natali Isabellae

quot uera atque hiemes, amica, et aestus
post nos liquimus a diebus illis
cum primum timido mihi Isabella
cognita est! Coma erat fere aurea, alto
corpore ut Phaëtontidum sororum
micabant ueneres cupidinesque
paululum quae animum mouere possent.
propter hoc (puto) et arduis diebus
saeculi noui, ut aurum in aurea arca,
nostra amicitia integra inuenitur.

Nouocomi, XI die ante Kalendas Octobres MMII

Metre: Hendecasyllables

Translation: *On Isabella's Birthday*

> How many winters and summers, my friend, we left behind our shoulders, since those days when for the first time Isabella was introduced to me, who was so shy! Your hair was almost golden, in your body, as tall as Phaethon's sisters, gracefulness shone that could move my soul only a bit. That is why (I believe), even in the hard days of the new century, our friendship is still entire like gold in a golden case. Como, September 21st 2002

*   *   *

Steven Perkins

Steven Perkins is the 2014 Indiana Teacher of the Year, the author of numerous articles and books including *Latin for Dummies* and *Achilles in Rome: The Latin Iliad of Baebius Italicus*, and an ancient Roman re-enactor. He currently teaches Latin at North Central High School in Indianapolis, Indiana.

4 Haiku

Steven writes: Some years ago I ran across the book *Tonight They All Dance: 92 Latin & English Haiku* (ed. Sacré and Smets, 1999). Since then I have incorporated Latin Haiku into my Latin III class. For more than two millennia, the Latin language and its literature have helped shape and reflect humanity. Haiku, a relative newcomer to the stage of world literature, is but a little over four hundred years old. Yet, their eventual joining seems inevitable. As the primitive settlement of Romulus expanded, it adopted and adapted elements of the surrounding cultures. Menander and Homer found their literary offerings recast in Plautus and Virgil, and Cicero would surely not have so endangered his life in the *Philippics* had he not had Demosthenes for a predecessor. Though the days of Roman territorial conquest are past, Latin does not weep with Alexander, for there are still literary worlds, if not to conquer, then to embrace. The beauty, clarity, and precise yet ethereal quality of Haiku have made it an attractive genre in which modern Latinists can try their hand.

(1)

> *emit puella*
> *ignota ab omnibus*
> *cibum in foro*

(2)

> *in turba ludunt*
> *pueri, oratore*
> *habente causam*

(3)

> *Autumno uirgo*
> *dolet mensem Iunium*
> *nouum transitum*

(4)

> *seruus captus in*
> *proelio prius miles*
> *timeo noua*

Metre: Haiku

127

Translations:

(1)

> Ignored by them all
> a young girl purchases food
> in the marketplace.

(2)

> In the crowd play young
> boys as the orator pleads
> his case in the court.

(3)

> A maiden in fall
> grieves that another season
> of marriage has passed.

(4)

> Captured as a slave
> in battle, I, a soldier,
> fear uncertainty.

Originally published in 'The Heresy of Latin Haiku', *Classical Bulletin*, Volume 78, Number 1, 2002, pp. 67-68.

*   *   *

Michiel Sauter

Michiel Sauter teaches German, Dutch and Latin in Nijmegen, the Netherlands.

Salax Taberna

Michiel writes: This is a poem about the owner of a filthy pub inspired by Catullus' poem 37 on a salax taberna.

> *cur cauponis olet salax taberna?*
> *tenax iste negat lauare caudam;*
> *manus mane lauat bis in matella*
> *deinde tergit eas ter in capillis*
> *ouo caluior est et iste caupo.*
> *num miraris eo magis rogasque*
> *quare fetida sit taberna putra?*

Metre: Hendecasyllables

Translation:

> Why does the publican's filthy pub stink?
> Tenaciously he refuses to wash his penis;
> in the morning he washes his hands in the chamber pot twice
> then he wipes them in his hair three times
> that publican is even balder than an egg.
> Do you really wonder and all the more ask
> why his dirty pub is stinking?

*   *   *

Venustas et Vetustas

Michiel writes: This poem is based on a true story about a bright young woman who went scantily clad to a job interview. She got the job and proudly posted pictures online of herself with her new, yet slightly older employer.

> *quid clamitabas? te putasne delectam*
> *ob indolem uel magnitudinem solum?*
> *o gratulemur! o puella uersuta!*
> *apparuisti seminuda patrono*
> *nam uix papillas uix natesque uelasti.*

tu foeda non es, caecus ille nequaquam;
Di, num est uetustas fortior uenustate?

Metre: Choliambic

Translation:

> Why were you shouting out loud? Do you think you have been chosen
> just because of your talent or your brightness?
> Oh congratulations! Oh cunning girl!
> You showed up half-naked before your employer,
> hardly hiding your breasts and buttocks.
> You are not ugly, he is by no means blind.
> Oh Gods, old age is not stronger than beauty, is it?

*   *   *

Massimo Scorsone

Massimo Scorsone the former editor of *Parthenias* – Collection of Neo-Latin Poetry, is currently member of the Scientific Committee of *SuRSUm* Interdepartmental Centre for Scholarly Aids in Humanities (University of Turin) and chief editor of the *Corona Patrum Erasmiana* for the *CESU* – European Centre of Humanistic Studies. In the field of Latin – as well as sometimes of Greek – composition, till today he has published very little, although several of his *pastiches* are already available on the Web in 'pro-manuscripto' form.

Eoan Airs for Hesperian Strings

Poetry by definition is untranslatable.
Only creative transposition is possible.
ROMAN JAKOBSON

Massimo writes: My first attempt at freely paraphrasing in Latin – and, as I do confess, in an ingenuous, albeit somewhat Borgesian fashion – some acceptable specimens of Old Chinese poetry was only a few years ago.[1] However, this oriental bee had been buzzing in my bonnet for a good while, at least from the bygone days of my youth when 'my eyes', to use the words of Captain Charles Ryder, 'were dry to all save poetry'. As an adolescent, mere omnivorous curiosity first led me to some of the most celebrated collections of Chinese verse in various Italian and French renditions, then to English and German translations,[2] and thus I envisioned the possibility of *Latine*, or even *Graece* moulding some exemplary imitations of the originals, and in the same rich vein of a poetic tradition that is as classical as ours, yet so different from the one to which the western *Institutio Studiorum* has accustomed us.[3] My labours continued to produce a fair amount of hotchpotch, even when I at last decided to shed the guise of the learned translator, rather surreptitiously invoking the authority of (more or less) recent precursors to justify the Orientalism *en travesti* of my 're-creations'.[4]

In fact, the pieces I have occasionally gleaned from those fields as a 'bad Laverna of good poetry',[5] though abounding in the untranslatable, are less a deliberate product of personal craftsmanship than the effect of an interpreting (or counterfeiting, if you prefer) practice, primarily intended for my own use, as the only device which enables me to partly understand literary works – and their underlying linguistic and cultural ethos – otherwise impervious to the guileless amateur wandering in the Sinological domain.

Thus, although there is much in Chinese poetry that is readily enjoyable – from the sheer, fanciful elegance of Immortal Li Po to Tu Fu's warm yet discreet tenderness, to the courteous idyllic allusiveness of Wang Wei and P'ei Ti, and so on – and immediately touches responsive chords within us, even when we are unaware of the original framework of its stylistic conventions, manifest efforts had to be made to adapt the selected prosodical calque – sometimes more Catullan than Horatian in pattern – to the original register, eventually smoothing any too sharp 'Roman' traces but, at the same time, seeking not to lose the peculiarly, or even idiomatically Chinese imprint of the model, beyond any quaintness. I also tried to maintain a distinct tone for each poem, carefully dosing various suggestions, lyrical and elegiac, as seemed meet.[6]

Ultimately, I leave to the cultivated ear the task of perceiving, through the aforementioned game of mutual adjustments and correspondences, the echoes awakened by fleeting impressions on a merry-go-round of whirling chronotopes. Having bartered the Eoan *ch'in* for the Latian *barbitos*, I find that the Eastern Muses sing closer to my heart. And you, can you hear them too?

Notes:

1) At the beginning of the millennium, Marc Moskowitz of Arlington, MA hosted some of my 'fakes' on 'Poesis Latina Hodierna / Contemporary Latin Poetry', a website – already mentioned in previous issues – that 'is meant to be a jumping-off point for examples of modern [...] Latin verse' (see http://www.suberic.net/~marc/scorsone.html). I then published a few latinized adaptations of poems by Li Po in the form of another semi-forgery in *Vox Latina* 38, 148 (2002), pp. 183-191. Rather pompously entitled 'De Li Tai Po Clarissimo Sinorum poeta, speciminibus quibusdam ejus operis additis', this new essay of such a jocular inclination was indulgently tolerated by the editors, the late Prof. Fr. Caelestis Eichenseer, OSB and Dr. Sigrid Albert of Saarland University, and thus my paraphrases of Chinese verse were ascribed to a fictitious character – one Fr. Kuno Dühring-Ebner, SJ (Berlin 1862 - Peking 1927). Could he have been a pious kinsman of the German social philosopher Karl Eugen Dühring, of Marx/Engelsian memory? In fact, the allusion to an imaginary Jesuit Sinologist should be understood as a simple tribute of admiration for the early pioneers in Oriental Studies, who succeeded in combining a traditional humanistic education with the capacity to penetrate the soul of the Middle Kingdom's literature.

2) Only recently (but not without the friendly help of some initiates and a bit of Ezrapoundian boldness) did I dare face the tangle of the ideograms – a true *selva selvaggia* to the trespasser.

3) I then resolved, as my whimsy took me, to adopt the Ionic dialect only to transpose the venerable, though anonymous, poems and ballads of the Confucian *Shih-king*, or 'Book of Odes'. But why 'translate' anything from Classical Chinese into Greek, or Latin? Far from simply being arbitrary snobbery, or the serendipitous result of an impressionistic choice (even if, after all, humanistic Latin, with its soft, timeless indeterminacy, its versatile expressiveness and capability, would seem particularly suitable for such a task), it was an option inspired by a certain compelling analogies between these classical tongues: for they can universally be considered, in fact, as written 'mandarin' idioms, marked (a merely fortuitous convergence) not only for their many peculiarities – from 'their tendency to transcend the limits of national boundaries and time' to 'their prestige, usually in contrast to a "vulgar" spoken medium; their irregular phonological evolution; their role as vehicle for and symbol of a transmitted cultural tradition' –, which *propter similitudinem* we ascribe as a rule to such literary codes, and that can only in part be 'explained as characteristic of written languages in general', but also on account of other important, and perhaps more structural aspects, including 'their reputed resistance to change' (thus far Richard A. Kunst, 'Literary Chinese Viewed in the Light of Literary Latin' [a previously unpublished comparative essay, available online in both PDF/html versions from the website of the Humanities Computing Laboratory of Durham, NC:
see http://www.humancomp.org/ftp/yijing/litchinese_in_light_of_litlatin.pdf
or http://www.humancomp.org/ftp/yijing/litchinese_in_light_of_litlatin.html]).

4) See Massimo Scorsone, 'Serica Delecta. Cinque cimenti parafrastici', *Semicerchio - Journal of Comparative Poetry* 4 (2006), pp. 37-40 (the contribution, containing parallel Chinese/Latin texts, is easily readable or even downloadable in PDF version at:
http://www.unisi.it/semicerchio/upload/sc34_scorsone.pdf).

5) D. Magnus Ausonius, *Epist.* 14.104 (*'Bonorum mala carminum Laverna'*). A feminine deity of the Netherworld, probably of Etruscan origin, Laverna was imagined by the Quirites as 'patroness of gain, good or bad, and so the goddess of thieves' (Hugh G. Evelyn White).

6) Please note, however, that these neo-Latin rearrangements from Old Chinese poems are meant simply to be 'reading texts', i.e. as literature intended only for pleasure, or enjoyment reading. Therefore, the numerous footnotes and discussions you might expect to find in such texts are missing; in the same way, you will find here no indications of textual hermeneutics apart from those, which are shown, as it were, already crystallized in my interpretations. So, for that sort of things, if you do not wish to consult a standard scholarly edition of classical Chinese verse, you should visit websites or blogs dedicated to the subtle art of poetry translation from the Chinese, such as 'Classical Chinese Poems in English' (see: www.chinesepoemsinenglish.blogspot.com) or 'Chinese Poems in English', an online literary resource of the *Hong Kong Economic Journal* (see: http://www.hkej.com/template/blog/php/blog_index.php?blog_blogs_id=1751), both run by Andrew W.F. Wong, OBE, JP.

LEPORIVS (vulgo LI PO / LI BAI)

1. Fannio Chunio, Pierio Gentio, Congio Chophuo poëtis rursus ad montes redituris

> "tigridas ille nequit deprendere, siue leones
> retia qui lepori modo tendit,"
> caeruleis pleno delapsus nubibus ore
> prae latebras ita praeco canebat.
>
> o magne ingenio, Fanni, uir, sancte magister,
> et facili, probe Pierie, aeui
> integritate potis; praeclare at tu quoque, Congi,
> tot bene muneribus cumulate,
>
> deuoti nebulis, cultores aëris omnes,
> montanae super ardua pinus
> culmina mens frugi, cordataque robore uirtus,
> si gracilis prope, tollitur isto:
>
> una tribus lodix sat erat, dum caute grabatum
> sternitur accubitis spatiosa,
> hiberni fracta glacie qui flumina riui
> frigida saepius ore sumebant;
>
> sic pedibus senis, de consuetudine, binum
> sufficiebat item crepidarum

par, cum, ceu uario palantia nubila caelo,
quo libet, errabatis inanes.

mox autem nemorum, mandante antistite, lustra
deseruistis, et hospita saxa,
sibila tollentes, tenui per acumina ferri
constricta, pie coetus, abolla,

saltibus hesterna cui iam per somnia uastis
nocte redire iugoque uidetur.
otia harundifera lunae sub sidera cordi
ualle, uirenteque ludere cliuo;

atque Eoa Lycone uale, salueque bibentes
nuper ad ostia triste uicissim
extrema cellis deprompta cernimur urna
hinc discessuri, positaque.

at, quamquam gelido terrarum senta teguntur
uellere, et aspera, fitque caduca
lubrica canitie, dum ningit, equoque labante
semita uepribus abditur altis,

uester fumifici redolens ut caespitis herba
sit tamen ipse mihi memoratus,
quae neque uere suis ubicumque uaporibus aurae
aestifero neque tempore parcit.

Metre: Alcmanian strophe

Translation: *'But think about old friends the most... '*

'The hunter, who sets snares only for hares, cannot capture tigers or lions': So sang the herald, descending from the blue clouds, at the mouth of the rocky cave. O revered Han, a man of great intellect you are; and you, honest P'ei, you with all the frankness of youth; and you, too, eminent K'ung, with your many merits: ye devotees of the clouds, ye inhabitants of the heights, above the lofty top of the mountain pine this straight heart austere, this strenuous and stout virtue, though simple, is exalted by your patience: a single blanket was once enough to cover all three, when a wide stone was a bed to sleep; and often, you broke the ice on the mountain stream in winter, and drank its cold currents. For three pairs of feet, as was your custom, there were only two pairs of sandals when, light like vagrant clouds in the capricious sky, you wandered everywhere. But then, on the governor's orders, whistling you left the dark woods, and hospitable cliffs, ye happy fellows, dressed in lightweight capes closed with a sharp iron fibula. Last night, you dreamed you had returned there to the wide ravines, and the mountains (for you loved lounging by moonlight in the Valley of Bamboos, and in the

mountains green); and today here, in Lu, beside the Eastern Gate we
drank a sad toast, bidding each other a mutual adieu, once we had
emptied the bottle from the cellar. But though the white frost covers the
trees, and the blizzard makes the path, hidden by thick bushes, slippery
for the stumbling horse, your memory will be for me as fragrant as a tuft
of smoking grass: for, be it spring or summer, it ever exhales its perfume
through the air.

[A valedictory ode, addressed by Li Po (701-762 A.D.) to his fellow poets Han
Chun, P'ei Cheng and K'ung Ch'ao-fu when escorting them back to the
mountains.]

*   *   *

THEOCINETIVS (T'AO CH'IEN / TAO QIAN)

2. *Carmen Baccho subiciente vates meditatur*

nauiter crates casulae salignas
rure praecinctus, populisque texo,
paene plaustrorum strepitu silente,
    quadrupedumque.

iure quaerenti tamen haec, amice,
qua tibi detur fieri profabor:
namque cor totis procul hinc facessit
    rebus abactum,

donec obtutu Notiale longe
collis adparet, iuga densa, dorsum
saepta chrysanthos mihi colligenti
    propter Eoa.

dulce montana quoniam sub aura
iam magis lumen, pariterque primo
uesperi nidos repetunt uolucres
    compare nisu.

talibus sensus, reor, ac profundi
uis inest ueri uelut ipsa signis:
uerba rimantem simul et facultas
    deficit, et uox.

Metre: Sapphics

Translation: *In the Busy Quiet.* Kōan *Composed while Drinking Wine*

A wattle hut I weave in the countryside, among the peasantry; yet, wheels and mules stay silent. You ask me how I am able to work this miracle? My heart flies away from the world, Nature continues its course. Chrysanthemums at the eastern hedge I pick, while there, to the South, the distant hills turn blue, and in the peaceful shade of the mountain sweet comes the end of the day, as the birds return to their nests. These are the things that reveal the sense of what is real: speaking of them the voice fails, lacking words.

[The poem is the fifth in a series of twenty 'Drinking Songs' written by T'ao Ch'ien, or T'ao Yuan-ming, also known as 'Master Five Willows' (365-427 A.D.), one of the most renowned among the pre-Tang Chinese bards.]

*   *   *

TYPHOIVS (Tu Fu / Du Fu)

3. Domesticis nuntiis tandem acceptis, animum Musis aperiendo moestitiae ex tempore indulget

en, quas forte peragrante piis hospite, litterae,
ualde sollicitus iam manibus commiseram diu
dandas rite domum, sedibus a sordidulis licet
incultaque aliquando redierunt mihi de plaga,

optatisque quidem ex more refertae quoque nuntiis:
quas suspensus ego iure inopinas prope, et anxius,
spe nec denique deiectus, adhuc auspice litteras
dilectae caritate opperiebar subolis parens.

Vrsillus bene pro parte ualet, disque iuuantibus
nunc pulchre uiget, ac, teste tabella, puer omnium
est quem corde foues, Mannule mi, praeter et intimos,
fratres exsuperantem ingenii munere ceteros.

aerumnosa senectus nimium, cui solitudinis
aegre fertur onus! sed trepidis ille molestior
curis angor, homo conficitur quo uagus, a suis
distentum miserae donec eum praepediant morae.

quid uero facerem? aut quid faciam? pessima tempora
distractis modo nos officiis esse simul uetant.
quondam namque, capillo satis incanus, erilibus

irrepsi laribus, sceptra salutatum oriens; rotas

mox sacras subii, Caesareo numine concitus,
phoenicemque; suis attamen urbs imperii potens
atque excelsum Aquilonis caput umbris minime caret,
limes dum niueis Hesperius candicat imbribus.

et, grassante magis iam Borea, saepius aduena
huc anser reuolat stridulus, udusque feracibus
tot pisces pluuiis annus alit, turbidula satos
unda, sedula nec linquit iners munia uillicus,

intenta procul accliue solum qui subigit manu
uel deserta fere pensilibus ruribus edita.
supremum o utinam sic obeam, non aliter, diem :
arrepto, mihi sors si qua sinit prouida, pastino.

Metres: Fifth Asclepiadean

Translation: *Reflections in Melancholy*

Thus, at last, has come the answer to the letter I so long ago entrusted to the pious hands of a guest, so that he carry it to my home; thus, finally, a reply has come to me, though sent from a poor land, from a village wild. It is welcome, nonetheless, rich as it is with its load of news, for until now I had awaited it with the bated breath of an anxious parent, unable as I was to hope too much, and yet still trusting in the love of my dear children: Bear Cub is fine, I learn, and, with the gods' blessing, is growing up healthy; and thus he, my dear Pony Boy, according to your words is the best-loved of your brothers, the cleverest of them all. Ah, how painful is old age for those, whose hearts ache with loneliness! Yet, it is more excruciating still for the trembling worries and distress under which the man oppressed must labour in exile, whilst bitter troubles keep him from his home. Then, what should I have done? Or what should I do, now? Hard times and our different obligations prevent us from being together. Once, in fact, hoary-haired already, I came to the Palace to pay my tributes to the majesty of the Emperor; then, as he commanded, I followed the sacred chariot with its phoenix-embroidered pavilion; now, however, the capital city of the Kingdom, the northern supreme seat is populated by none but ghosts, while the western border is whitening beneath the snow storms; and I see come here, as the north wind rages ever more frequently, the shrilling wild duck, while the wet year with fertile rainfall brings fish, the spawn of muddy waves. Yet, here the industrious farmer neglects none of his work, he who expertly cultivates his hills, his terraced fields, now almost deserted. Oh, but thus may I end my life, and not otherwise! If luck abide with, thus wish to die, hoe in hand.

[A homesick epistle by Tu Fu (712–770), thus celebrating the birthday of his newborn. 'Bear Cub' and 'Pony Boy' are nicknames the poet gave to two of his sons, Tsung-wu and Tsung-wen respectively.]

137

VANNEIVS et PAETIVS (WANG WEI, P'EI TI / BEI DI)

Ex Amnicis Vanae amoebaeis

4. Agger Arundinum Abundans

[Vanneius:]

> celsa cadente nitent sub diuo gramina sole
> aethera dum referunt, siluaque densa uiget,
> et lento trepidant undantibus horrida motu
> caerula pro foliis, arboreumque mare:
> nescio quis Sancum petit – an lignator? –, operta
> solus per saltus auia calle means.

[Paetius:]

> itque suis sub colle reditque ambagibus amnis
> iamiam albente piger, pronior inde, face.
> ad cliuum uiridis crebrescit arundine multa
> pergenti, frondis dein tenuatur honor:
> absque mora, placidus, resonante canore, supinum
> montis iter teneo, culmina nota tuens.

Metre: Elegiacs.

Translation: *Amoebaean Couplets I: The Range of the Bamboo Sea*

> [Wang Wei:] At sunset, the light from the sky is reflected over the high verdant ridge of thriving bamboo woods, and the leaves' deep blue sways in soft waves, like a sea of fronds. Invisible, someone ascends alone, along hidden tracks, the slope toward Mount Shang – perhaps a woodcutter. No one knows.

> [P'ei Ti:] Here and there, already whitening in the moonlight, the meandering river flows: slowly at first, then faster, while the green bamboo grove thickens, though further along thins. Thus, tirelessly, I keep on climbing my mountain path: and I sing, as I walk, the familiar mountain peaks fixed in my sight.

[From the collection of the 'Wang River Poems', or better 'Antiphonal Songs': something like the lyrical trophies of a gentle competition between Wang Wei (699-759 A.D.) and his *confrère* P'ei Ti (c. 714-? A.D.) about several idyllic topics. I am grateful to Andrew Wang-Fat Wong (Huang Hongfa), *vir litteris adprime imbutus*, for the help he gave me, providing a felicitous interpretation of the poem's ambiguous title.]

* * *

5. Piperis Arboretum

[Vanneius:]

> hanc clarae suboli casia fragrante salutem,
>   ecce, propinantes dicimus, atque scypho,
> per me sincero dum florida datur amico
>   malua, piperque super gemmea prata merum
> offertur (procliue suis de nubibus o si
>   huc daemon planta conuolet ipse leui!).

[Paetius:]

> attamen hi rubeis tunicatos, optime, dumi
>   uepribus, et spina nos remorantur acri.
> dulcis odoratis circum te funditur aura
>   turibus; ut graderis, spirat aroma uia.
> te cortinarum facient tua fata potentem:
>   suauia sic costi semina, domne, legas!

Metre: Elegiacs

Translation: *Amoebaean Couplets II: The Pepper Tree Grove*

[Wang Wei:] Let us drink now, with cups of fragrant cassia, a toast to illustrious offspring, whilst I give mauve flowers to my true friend, offering him peppercorns over the green grass carpet (oh if only thou, venerable spirit, would descend from thy clouds!).

[P'ei Ti:] This bramble hampers us, however, most esteemed sir, catching our clothes with its red thorns, with its sharp spines, while perfumes and scents follow thee as thou pass. To govern the tripods is indeed thy destiny: thus may thou gather, my lord, the augural seeds of sweet-smelling Saussurea.

[The poem is filled with mythical references and symbols, after the manner of Ch'ü Yüan's (c. 332-295 a. C.) elegies. Thus, e.g., the aforementioned 'illustrious offspring' – alluding to the daughters of the legendary Emperor Yao – hints at the high-mindedness of the wise. In the same allegorical imagery, spices and aromatic plants denote virtues, while the 'red thorns' stand for 'daily life', etc.]

*   *   *

SOSIBIVS (SU TUNG-P'O / SU DONGPO)

6. Nocturna inter pocula, ad amicum

> o nitidum tacitis, argentea nox, decus sub astris!
>   quid aptius nam, candicante luna,
> dulce merum genio quam fundere, comiterque paucis
>   pocilla largus ingerens amicis,

gaudia testari cordis pia? gloriosus ergo,
sequestre laude, falsa ne requiras
famae dona, uorax neu praemia, stulta quae bonorum
tam fluxa semper appetit cupido:

prona quidem in nihilum, ceu somnia uana; ceu tepentes
ab igne, frigent quae modo, fauillae
languidus in cineres ut abit uapor; ilicet fugaces
micantis, immo, ceu facis tenebrae.

quid, uel summa, tibi sapientia, quaeue disciplinae,
beatitatem dum cupis serenam?
quin sibi fausta, umbris sine lumina cuique comprecanti
satis, superque nuda sit uoluptas.

ipse itaque, ipse domum cum serius, ocius reuertar,
nil praeter album nubium maniplum
forte ferens umeris ego, dulceque pectinem sonantem,
plenamque testam laetus hinc abibo.

Metre: Fourth Archilochian

Translation: *A Toast by Moonlight: To Happiness*

What glorious brightness, oh silver night, beneath this starry sky! What could be better, when the pale Moon shines, than toasting the genius with sweet wine, and witnessing the simple happiness of your heart, as you kindly fill the cups, like a bounteous host ministering to a few friends? Thus, full of pride, long not fame's false gifts, deceitfully pimped by praise! And, in the same way, hunger not for ephemeral prizes, for those things, which the foolish greed for goods ever desires: things that are next to nothing, as vain as dreams, or ashes from a bonfire, warm at first, but soon cold, when the smoke turns slowly to powder; or like shades that flee at the first gleam of light. What is the use of wisdom, even as you strive to climb her summits? What serve its sciences and arts, if you only seek the happiness of a peaceful life? For to all those who seek days serene, without shadows, a simple delight is more than enough. I myself, when sooner or later go home, will take with me nothing but a bunch of white clouds, a sweet-singing *ch'in*, and a wine-filled jar.

[A charming 'Drinking Poem' composed by poet, scientist and statesman Su Shi, a.k.a. Su Tung-p'o (1037-1101 A.D.), the 'Gay Genius' (Lin Yutang) flourished under the Sung Dynasty.]

*   *   *

Nicholas Stone

Nicholas Stone is a Classicist studying at Westminster School in London, who enjoys versifying in Latin, Greek and English.

Distichon De Placentis

Nicholas writes: Given the rather odd content of this distich, some explanation ought to be supplied: it sums up a story told to me this year by my grandfather, relating how when he walked home from work at night he often passed by what he thought was a patisserie, with cakes in the window. He eventually went in, in the daytime, only to discover that it was a dental practice, and that the 'cakes' were in fact sets of false teeth!

> *semper nocte domum quando ibam liba uidebam;*
> *nunc uideo dentes irradiante die!*

Metre: Elegiac couplet

Translation:

> I always saw cakes as I walked home by night;
> Now I see teeth by the day shining bright!

*　　*　　*

Tax Avoidance

Nicholas writes: I wrote this distich, along with some celebratory verses for various people attending, for Westminster School's Election Dinner of 2015, an annual occasion at which epigrammatic verse is read aloud, containing translingual puns on topical subjects or persons. As I wrote it during the debate on tax havens, this one features the puns "non dom", "tax" and "Osborne" (referencing our many-wiled Chancellor).

> *non Dominus terrae qui contrahit axe tributum.*
> *per populos bona erunt plurima carpit homo.*

Metre: Elegiac couplet

Translation:

> The Good Lord doesn't tax the folks above.
> Men here, though; taxing us is what they love!

*　　*　　*

Richard Sturch

Richard Sturch is a retired clergyman of the Church of England who read Classics at school and at University, but had only sporadic contact with neo-Latin thereafter. He has translated Tolkien's *The Lord of the Rings* into Latin as *Erus Anulorum*.

Two Verses from Erus Anulorum

Richard writes: It was in 2004 that I contributed a light-hearted piece, about the problems that would be involved in translating *The Lord of the Rings* (which I have loved ever since it came out) into Latin, to a collection on *Translating Tolkien* (and later to a *Festschrift* for my former Classics master's 84th birthday). In it I regretted that the great work would probably never be undertaken; but then something said to me "Why not try it yourself?" I have been at it, off and on, for about six years, and have just finished Book Four. Whether it will be a *magnum opus* or merely what Tacitus called a *magna moles et improspera* remains to be seen.

The verses have been the real challenge. Metre should vary according to subject – and in the case of *LOTR*, species. Hobbits and Dwarves, I felt, would use accentual metres like the 'Goliardic' I have used for Frodo's song at Bree ('There is an inn, a merry old inn'). But Elves, and Men of Gondor, would be more classically-minded; so Galadriel's *Lament* is in straight hexameters. The Men of Rohan composed their songs in alliterative verse, and I think any Latin version will have to take that form too, despite lack of precedent. (I haven't tried this yet!) And Tom Bombadil actually talks in a kind of loose English hendecasyllables; there was no real choice there, loose hendecasyllables it had to be in Latin.

(1) Frodo's song, 'There is an inn, a merry old inn ...'

sub uetusto colle stat hilaris taberna
qua talem ceruisiam porrigit pincerna
ut olim Vir uenerit Lunae de lucerna
ut sitis sedata sit sua sempiterna.

agasoni feles est, saepe temulenta,
modulatur fidibus uia uiolenta ,
quarum sonus euocant nunc delectamenta,
tunc in altis uocibus stridulis tormenta.

caupo canem aluit, callidum odorum,
paruae magnitudinis, cupidum iocorum;
hospitum qui auscultat uerba facetorum
emittitque obloquens risum indecorum.

142

bos hic quoque pascitur cornibus ornata,
reginis superbior dum sit tranquillata,
sed cum fidis carmine fiat fascinata
tum saltantis fluctuat cauda capillata.

aptum est armarium argenti catinis,
aptus cocleariis apothecae finis;
honorantur feriae instrumentis binis
quae ministri poliunt horis matutinis.

potiones maximas Lunae Vir potabat,
fidibusque stridulis feles ululabat,
lanx cum cocleario hilare saltabat,
uacca quoque, dum canis caudam indagabat.

tum exhausto poculo Vir nunc satiatus
subter sellam uoluitur potu superatus,
somnians ceruisiam, axis dum stellatus
rediente aurora pallescit lustratus.

feli tunc est agaso anxie locutus
"frena mandunt lunares equi dum solutus
dormit erus somnians sub sellam uolutus;
mox resurget et dies anceps et acutus!"

carmen modulata est resuscitaturum
quale posset mortuis reddere futurum;
donec caupo hospiti donat ictum durum:
"excitare! mane adest diem adlaturum!"

Lunae Virum languidum omnes sustulere;
equi albi lunares pone aduenere;
bos ut cerua exsultans noluit manere;
ipsae ex armario lances cucurrere.

magis magis rapide fides resonabant,
canis paruus latrabat, patinae saltabant,
bos et equi inuerso in capite stabant,
excitati hospites in solo saltabant.

ruptis cunctis fidibus lyra crepitauit!
bos trans Lunam siluit, coetus inhiauit;
risu canis ioculum talem aspectauit;

lancem, coclearium sonitus fugauit.

Luna lente uoluitur post collem morata,
ipsa Sol nunc oriens multum est mirata;
quamquam Solis coeperat lux desiderata,
omnes ad cubilia ibant adfectata!

*   *   *

(2) Galadriel's Lament, 'I sang of leaves, of leaves of gold'

cum de frondibus auratis cecini, creuere profecto:
cum de flaminibus, uenerunt carmine uenti.
Solem ultra Lunamque, maris qua spuma fluebat,
aurea crescebat longinqui litoris arbor
lustrata Eldamaris sub scintillantibus astris,
Quendorum speculae Tirionis moenia iuxta.
illic auriferas ramosus plurimus annus
frondes sustulerat; nos autem triste perennes
Oceanum citra lacrimis deflemus acerbis.
Lórien alma, dies hiberna aduentat ut omnes
deiciat frondes, quas flauas auehet amnis.
Lórien alma, exsul secreta haec litora noui
marcentique elanore diu diademata feci.
at si cantarem de nauibus, ecqua ueniret
me trans tam latum nauis uectura profundum?

Metre: (1) Goliardics, (2) Hexameters

Translations: From *The Lord of the Rings, The Fellowship of the Ring*, (1) Book I Chapter IX 'At the Sign of the Prancing Pony', (2) Book II Chapter VIII, 'Farewell to Lórien'. © J. R. R. Tolkien.

*   *   *

Saint Mark

Richard writes: On the occasion of the patron saint's Day (25th April) of the editor of this journal, I recalled a hymn in his honour written by Laurence Housman, brother of a celebrated editor of Lucan and Manilius, and published as #220 in *The English Hymnal*. It was obviously written with mediaeval Office Hymns in the back of the mind, so ...

qui primus Dei gratia
saluante scripsit de uita

euangelistae lumine
concelebramus hodie.

accensus igne Spiritus,
desiderauit animus
integra mente auditum
edere uerbum diuinum.

deinde clara deitas
illuminauit litteras
quae morientis etiam
solari possunt animam.

o sanctum cor, idoneum
scribere Uitam hominum!
praesentes quoque animi
monstrent exemplum Domini.

sic errantes inscitia
ducantur Marci doctrina,
ut posthac sint ab angelis
in uitae scripta tabulis.

laudate mundi Dominum,
qui nobis misit Filium,
et docuit per Spiritum
euangelistam pristinum.

*　　*　　*

Metre: Rythmic iambic

English original (© Laurence Housman, 1865-1959):

> The Saint who first found grace to pen
> The Life which was the Life of men,
> And shed abroad the Gospel's ray,
> His fame we celebrate today.
>
> Lo, drawn by Pentecostal fire,
> His heart conceived its great desire,
> When pure of mind, inspired, he heard
> And with his hand set forth the Word.
>
> Then, clearly writ, the Godhead shone
> Serene and fair to look upon;
> And through that record still comes power
> To lighten souls in death's dark hour.

O holy mind, for wisdom fit
Wherein that Life of lives stood writ,
May we through minds of like accord
Show forth the patterns of our Lord.

And so may all whose minds are dark
Be led to truth by good Saint Mark,
And after this our earthly strife
Stand written in the Book of Life.

Praise God Who made the world so fair,
And sent His Son our Savior there,
And by His Holy Spirit wist
To teach the first Evangelist.

*   *   *

Animus Aequus Philosophiae Expers

Richard writes: Back in 1959 Dr. Eric Mascall, then a Student of Christ Church, Oxford (later Professor of the History & Philosophy of Religion at KCL) produced a small book of verses called *Pi in the High*. One, 'Unphilosophic Contentment', was subtitled 'A Horatian Ode'; and not long after, while in the Army in Singapore, I sent a Latin version, in Sapphics, to my brother Nicholas. A few days ago Nicholas came across the letter containing it and sent me a photocopy. Dr. Mascall died in (I think) 1991. I attach his original verses, as well as my 1960 effort, but have no idea who inherited the copyright. I doubt whether he himself would have objected to their appearing in *Vates*; he was himself the author of a fine Latin parody of Thomas Aquinas.

Quinte, narrantur nisi falsa, sunt qui
dignitatis uix memores honestae,
quae patent nondum sibi praeterire
      rsse negarint;

his tamen magna pietate moti
esse respondent alibi futura
(uerba nos firmant ceterum legentes
      Herodotorum).

tertii forsan miseri supersunt;
uatibus parent, eademque credunt
falsa per sese, simul et secundum
      quid fore uera.

'ueritas non est inimica falsi!'
dictitant quidam: 'dialecticorum
dirigunt sanctas acies amicae

146

rite chororum!"

me sed infirmum neque mens perita
in loca eniti iubet altiora
passibus claudis, neque amore magno
    spiritus urget.

si quis errabit per agros deorum
carpet et fructus amaranthianos,
nonne egestatem mihi roly-poly
    cocta leuabit?

dum Iouis nectar sapientiores
Indicum uel soma bibunt beati,
me iuuant testae rubidi Falerni,
    somnus et aufert.

gaudiis tantis alii fruantur
quae creant grandes animi Platonum;
sat placet cenis mihi poculisque
    sumere uitam.

Metre: Sapphics

Translation: *Unphilosophic Contentment* © Eric Mascall

Friend, there are those, as I have heard,
Who, lost to sense of shame, insist
That that which has not yet occurred
Does not exist.

Others, more pious these, avow,
As history unerring tells,
That that which is not up to now
Is somewhere else.

While some, a sad priest-ridden crew,
Hold, or in darker ages did,
That what is false *per se* is true
Secundum quid.

Yet other some claim true and false
No foes, but each of each orectic,
United in the sacred waltz
Of dialectic.

Me feeble, of noetic strain
Nor able much nor over-fond,
Problems on this pneumatic plane
Are quite beyond.

147

Revering him whose spirit feeds
In fields of amaranth and moly,
I satisfy my simple needs
With roly-poly.

Content that souls heroic flow
On seas of nectar and of some,
I swill my bottled beer and so
Pass into coma.

Let others taste the heady joy
That comes with philosophic thinking.
My coarser hours let me employ
Eating and drinking.

*   *   *

Joseph Tusiani

Joseph Tusiani was born in Italy but emigrated to the USA in 1947. Before his retirement he taught at the City University of New York (Herbert H. Lehman College), at Fordham University, and was Director of the Catholic Poetry Society of America as well as Vice President of the Poetry Society of America. His extensive list of publications includes poetry in English, Italian and Latin – he has been hailed as the greatest living neo-Latin poet.

4 Unpublished Poems

Joseph writes: I wish to congratulate you on the brilliant idea of an online magazine wholly devoted to the composition of Latin verse. This is a most audacious enterprise that everybody should encourage, and, as you see, I immediately do so (gently spurred by my good friend Professor Dirk Sacré) with a humble submission of four still unpublished poems of mine, which I myself have hastily translated according to your demands.

(1) Gliris Somnus

> longum glis dormit somnum sub noctibus amplis,
> nil nisi uenturi cupiens miracula ueris.
> quantum illi inuideo! uellem uelut ille beate
> dormire et lucis certus remanere diei.
> humanus somnus turbatur sensibus ipsis
> qui semper uigilant illumque furore flagellant.
> paruule callide glis, si in somno somnia uoluis,
> nil certe cernis nisi pulchrum uer rediturum
> dum longam ignoras hiemem tenebrasque niuesque
> mortali generi, tam longe a te, minitantes.
> dissimilem sortem mihi Fata aliena dederunt:
> paulum dormio et in somno est sol crastinus anceps.

(2) Fabula Nota

> fabula nota mihi est quae dulci in nomine Christi
>   praecedens astrum in nocte canit magica.
> illa nocte Puer diuus pastoribus imis
>   splendet, dum regum munera aperta iacent.
> fabula nota, ignota mihi hac aetate uideris
>   isto annoque redis: credere difficile est.
> sed suaue est ueterem dulcedinem eam memorari

149

quando mi puero uita facillima erat.

(3) Alae

alae, uastae alae iuuenis sublime poetae
somnium erant. hodie non est sub sole uolatus:
nunc duo crura mihi remanent infirma et inepta
quae longum reddunt de porta in portam iter omne.
hos quoque rade, senex, uersus quibus ultima gesta
tempora non possunt fieri quae prima fuere.
de terra te ipsam dele, mea uana senecta,
aut propriis alis spatium da liberum et amplum.

(4) In Memoriam Sebastiani

nondum te uidi in somno, defuncte sodalis,
nec mihi dixisti quod nunc cognoscis ab alto.
sed, mihi crede, tuam uocem imploro anxius, in te
fraterne fidens. oh, longus transiit annus
et tam longa fuit uana expectatio amici.
quid cito colloquium nostrum impedit? est Deus ipse
nil nisi uasta silens aeterna incognita moles?
interea tempus memini tranquillum et amatum
quando ad me prompte ueniebas uespere quoque
ut tecum exirem ad zephyri flamen capiendum
aut ad ludendas chartas, hostes sed amici.
uincebas semper sed perdere erat mihi gratum.
uincere, perdere: quid sunt haec certamina uitae
in mortis facie? et quid mors, quid uiuere, quid nos?
uerbum expecto tuum de caelo nunc tibi noto.

Josephus Tusiani, Novi Eboraci, Idibus Octobris MMX

Metres: Hexameters (1, 3, 4), Elegiacs (2)

Translations:

(1) The Sleep of a Dormouse

A dormouse sleeps his lengthy sleep through endless nights,

desiring nothing but the wonders of forthcoming Spring.
How I envy him! Like him, I, too, would like to sleep in bliss,
remaining in the certainty of the light of day.
But man's sleep is disturbed by our very senses,
ever awake, ever ruthlessly assailing it.
O clever little dormouse, if in your sleep you have dreams,
nothing, I'm sure, you see but the beauty of Spring that comes back,
meanwhile ignoring long winter and darkness and snows
threatening the human kind far away from you.
Hostile Fate granted a diverse lot to me:
Little I sleep, and even in my sleep the morrow's sun is uncertain.

(2) A known Fable

I know well the fable that, in Christ's sweet name announcing a star,
sings in the magical night.
In that very night a heavenly Babe shines before kneeling shepherds
while gifts of kings lie open before them.
O well-known fable, you seem unknown at my age, and unknown
return to me this year: it is so hard to believe!
And yet what peace to remember that ancient innocence
when life was so easy to the child that was I.

(3) Wings

Wings, ample wings were a poet's lofty dream.
There is no flight today beneath the sun:
Now two sickly shaky legs remain to me,
which make the path from door to door a lengthy trip.
Erase, old man, these verses too, which fail to make new deeds
the times you once called first.
And erase yourself from earth, O futile old age,
or give free and ample room to the wings that are yours.

(4) In Memory of Sebastian

I have not yet seen you in my dream, dear by-gone friend,
nor have you told me of what you have learned of the world above.
Believe me, your voice I anxiously expect with fraternal trust.
Oh, a full long year has elapsed, and as long a friend's expectation has
been.

What suddenly impedes our colloquy? Is God himself
Nothing but a silent, vast, unknown, eternal massiveness?
In the meantime I recall the tranquil happy days
when every evening punctually you came to my house
and forced me to go out with you for some fresh air
or to play cards as foes while still great friends.
You won every time and I did not mind to lose.
To win, to lose: in the presence of death what do such struggles mean?
And what is death, what is life, what are we?
I still expect a word about the place you now know well.

*   *   *

151

Webicus Bacchus

Joseph writes: I have recently heard of a new on-line magazine, called *BACCHUS*, soon to appear in Italy. The idea of Bacchus online inspired my *Webicus Bacchus*, which I am almost sure will raise a smile.

> *retibus et liquidis laqueis, Dionyse, dedisti*
> *ebrietatem animi mentisque viris super orbem.*
> *nunc grate genus humanum tribuit tibi donum –*
> *rete immane et deciduum quo tu quoque nosces*
> *ebrietatem hominum vivam sine te, sine vino.*
> *Webicus es Bacchus talisque per aeva manebis,*
> *sed semper, Dionyse, veni bona pocula portans.*

Metre: Hexameters

Translation:

By snares and liquid traps you, Dionysus, gave drunkenness of soul and mind to men on the earth. Now the grateful human race bestows on you a gift – a vast and falling net by which you also shall know that the drunkenness of men thrives without you, without wine. You are Online Bacchus and such you will remain through the ages, but always, Dionysus, come bearing pleasant cups.

*   *   *

Pro Senectute Mea

Joseph writes: I take the liberty of sending you these few lines. They help me to reconcile my eighty-eighth birthday with this glorious Easter Sunday. [Written Easter, 2011]

> *imbecille meum est senile corpus*
> *ut sulcata cutis reuelat oclis.*
> *multi, ergo, iuuenes, meum uidentes*
> *gressum lentum, animam putant inertem*
> *et mentem mediis iacentem in umbris.*
> *et fiat! sed amor, iuuentus, ardor*
> *quid sint et ualeant scio et recordor*
> *dum mundi memini uerenda cuncta.*
> *nolite, o iuuenes, uidere finem*
> *diuae mentis in hac humo caduca:*
> *aeternum uiget ac triumphat in me*
> *lucis principium quod in tenaci et*
> *una reste ligat senem et puellum.*

Metre: Hendecasyllables

Translation:

> My feeble body is old, as furrowed skin reveals to the eyes. Hence many youths seeing my slow step think that my soul is stagnant and that my mind is lying in the midst of shadows. And let it be so! But love, youth, passion – what they are and are worth I know and remember while I recall all the wonders of the world. Don't, o youths, see the end of a divine mind in this doomed earthly being. Eternity thrives and triumphs in me, the beginning of light which in one tenacious cord binds both the old man and the boy.

*   *   *

Ad Marcum Editorem

Joseph writes: These few hexameters sound quite facetious, but to me they are quite serious.

> *Marce, labore tuo, quo Vates colligis omnes,*
> *ignotos homines socios facis atque sodales,*
> *ex istis unus, Robertus Zisk tibi carus,*
> *nunc meus est subito factus pretiosus amicus.*
> *nil de illo nosco: si felix uiuat in urbe*
> *an uiridi in prato plantas numeret sibi notas;*
> *si magnum ostentet corpus plateae populosae*
> *an parvus gracilisque inter celsos uideatur.*
> *sed totum de illo scio: uir pius est si in terra*
> *prompte consimilis lacrimas uult tergere nati,*
> *si tantum sola uirtute Poeseos affers,*
> *PRO PRETIO PACIS te nuncupo, Marce, libenter.*

Metre: Hexameters

Translation:

> Mark, by your work, in which you bring together every unknown poet and make them friends and companions, one dear to you, Robert Zisk, has now suddenly become my cherished friend. I know nothing about him: whether he lives happily in a city, or counts as his own the well-known plants in a green meadow; whether he exhibits a large body on the crowded street, or seems small and gracious among the lofty. But I know everything about him: he is a worthy man if he desires unhesitatingly to wipe away the tears of a fellow being on this earth. If you can obtain so much by the sole power of Poetry, willingly, Mark, I nominate you for the Nobel Prize for Peace.

*   *   *

Lorenzo Viscido

Lorenzo Viscido was born in 1952 at Squillace, Southern Italy. He obtained his Doctor's Degree in Classical Literature from the University of Salerno in 1976 and for a few years taught Italian and Latin in some High Schools. He also was a researcher at the Department of Classics of the same University from 1979 to 1980 and at the University of Calabria from 1980 to 1981. In 1981 he left Italy in order to teach Italian and Latin at the "Scuola d'Italia" in New York City. He is the author of several books on Cassiodorus and many articles about the same author, as well about Clemens of Alexandria, Saint Jerome, Paul the Deacon and Byzantine hymnography. Several of his Latin poems have been published in *Vox Latina*, *Meander*, and *Latinitas*. He received *publicae laudes* at the *Certamen Vaticanum* of 1983 and 1986, the Gold Medal at that of 1985 and the Silver Medal at the *Certamen Catullianum* of 1984.

Dormi, Mater

Lorenzo writes: This poem is a short elegy in memory of my mother, who passed away on July 5th, 2012.

> non iam pocillum, mater dilecta, cafei
> te poterit somni soluere compedibus.
> namque in perpetuum tua pallida lumina clausit
> potio caelestis, dulce parata tibi.
> nunc dormi, mater; numquam sed sola manebis
> aeterna requie languida membra leuans.
> cernere quam laeto cyparissus corde solebas
> iamdudum tandem sit tua grata comes.

Metre: Elegiacs

Translation:

No more, beloved mother, will a cup of coffee be able to unchain you from the bonds of sleep. In fact a heavenly drink, sweetly prepared for you, closed for ever your pale eyes.

Now sleep, mother; but you'll never remain alone restoring for all eternity your weak limbs. A cypress, that for long time you used to watch with joy, will finally be your lovable companion.

*   *   *

154

Monita

Lorenzo writes: This poem, here and there now retouched, was already published in my *libel* entitled *Poematia* (Soveria Mannelli 1987).

> numquam consimiles tibi, mortalis, bene nosces
>   perbene ni cordis noueris ima tui.
> numne potest Musae quisquam sentire calorem
>   si uatum in cantum permanet usque rigens?
> nec pietate hominum poteris gaudere parumper
>   illûm ni totiens uerbera passus eris:
> umbris quot caelum nocturnis ante tenetur
>   lumine quam roseo grata resurgat Eos?
> cuidam concedas tandem benefacta caueto:
>   qui bene cumque facit, crimina multa creat.

Metre: Elegiacs

Translation: *Counsels.*

You'll never know, mortal, those who belong to your same race if you'll not know very well the depth of your heart. Can somebody feel the warmth of the poetry if he is always cold towards the singing of the poets?

Nor will you have the possibility to enjoy a little of men's pity if you'll not endure so often their hits: of how many shadows the sky is covered before the pleasant dawn rises again with its rosy light?

Finally don't give benefits to anybody: who does good, commits many crimes.

*   *   *

Mark Walker

Mark Walker (@vatesthepoet) is the editor of *Vates*. As his quite remarkably insightful biography on Amazon states, "Forced to earn a pittance so that he can clothe his 35 children in squalid rags and feed them boiled cabbages, Mark has recently translated into Latin J.R.R. Tolkien's *The Hobbit* (as *Hobbitus Ille*, HarperCollins, 2012), and translated from Latin into English verse Geoffrey of Monmouth's 12th-century poem *Life of Merlin* (Amberley Publishing, 2011), for which Herculean labours he has so far received little praise from an indifferent world." As a penance for his many and varied crimes (probably) he currently occupies the post of Head of Classics at a Preparatory School near London. But he'd much rather be playing his mandolin or Rickenbacker bass.

Quid Dicat Ille?

Mark writes: A question I would like all devotees of ancient teachers to ask themselves.

> *quid dicat ille rector et magisterque*
> *uestri, quid, ipse nobilis vir, admiror,*
> *quid, si uolubilesque uerba spargentes*
> *uos audiat uetusta, de suis priscis*
> *uerbis loquentes, de suis profundisque*
> *sententiis, itemque de sua mente?*
> *satis benigna uerba, sat, puto, docta*
> *olim fuisse, nec tamen satis certa:*
> *praecepta recte sed modesta narrata,*
> *a posteris piis in arduas sancte*
> *fides pieque nunc fideliter uersa:*
> *quid dicat ille dux modestus admiror?*

Metre: Scazons ('Limping' iambics)

Translation:

> I wonder what would he say, that teacher and guide of yours, that noble man, if he could hear you loudly spreading his dignified words, talking about his ancient pronouncements, about his profound opinions, even about his own mind? They were once reasonably good-natured words, I suppose, and learned too, but not so dogmatic; precepts delivered truthfully but modestly, now by pious posterity piously and faithfully transformed into a hard faith: what would he say, I wonder, that modest leader?

*   *   *

Dinosauria

Mark writes: The origin of this silly piece was a metrical experiment using nothing but the Latin names of dinosaurs – *Tyrannosaurus Rex, Stegosaurus* etc – with the half-formed idea of finding a fun way to teach the basics of quantitative verse. But after playing around a little bit, I found myself writing a Sapphic ode – for the first time! – that, though hardly in the manner of Horace, does attempt at least to observe some Horatian conventions, such as *synaphea* (continuous scansion from one line to the next within each stanza), a regularly heavy fourth syllable, and occasional use of the weak *caesura* (unusually twice in the second stanza, following *talis ... qualis*). Each stanza is a single sense-unit/sentence (stanzas 3 and 4 connected by *et*). Un-Horatian are the deliberately 'gargantuan' words, including several unwieldy genitive plurals, in an attempt to give the piece a lumbering, dinosaur-like gait. The first two stanzas seem rather prosaic but things get interesting (and funnier, hopefully) in the third and fourth when you are asked to imagine being seized by a T. Rex. The jokey payoff comes right at the end. I have attempted a little bit of word-play in stanzas 3 and 4 with *lacertosum* ('muscular', meant ironically – how puny you actually are in the arms of the monster), *lacertarum* (*lacerta*, 'lizard') and *lacertis* (*lacertus*, 'upper arm'). Note also that the accusative + infinitive in the third stanza works both ways: you gazing at the bloody features of the T. Rex, it staring right back at you. In fact T. Rex's forearms were notoriously teeny and he couldn't really have held you in those arms at all. The word *species* is used in the Linnaean sense

Dinosaurorum species (scientes
inquiunt) olim fuerant per orbem:
rupibus ruptis fodiunt uatillis
    stemma stupendum.

mors quidem talis fuit ossearum
belluarum qualis ad usque nostrum
saeculum semper miserenda nobis
    et metuenda.

finge – te Regis manibus Tyranni
(sportulae causa) subito prehenso –
te lacertosum facies tueri
    sanguinolentas

et lacertarum, minimis lacertis
dentibus magnis, hilareque ridet
te, renidens atque boans, minutum
    Terribilis Rex.

ne queraris, ne doleas opertum
funus idcirco gregis opstupendae:
forte si saevae nihilo sepultae

te sepelissent!

Metre: Sapphics

Translation:

Species of dinosaurs, scientists say, once existed throughout the world: having broken open the rocks they unearth with their trowels an astonishing lineage. But the death of the bony monsters was such as up to our own time is still to be pitied and feared. Imagine – suddenly having been seized (for the sake of a snack) by the hands of the Tyrant King – imagine that brawny you catches sight of his gore-stained features [and vice versa], and the Terrible King of lizards, with the smallest arms and huge teeth, cheerfully laughs – grinning and bellowing – at tiny you. Do not lament, do not mourn therefore the mysterious funeral of the astonishing flock: if by chance the fierce creatures had not been buried, they would have buried you!

*   *   *

Ad Lunam

Mark writes: The great *Requiem* sequence, *Dies Irae*, has long exercised a special fascination for me – this in spite of, or possibly because of, my unbelief in matters spiritual (psychologists, discuss). Considered purely as poetry it has, I think, a passion and a power unrivalled in the whole *corpus* of not just medieval and sacred verse, but all Latin poetry. An opinion not entirely without precedent: Lord Macaulay once remarked that he thought *Quaerens me sedisti lassus* was 'the saddest line of poetry' he had ever read – this from a man who had read pretty much every known line of Latin and Greek verse. And when Dr. Johnson once protested to Mrs. Thrale that all religious verse was 'cold and feeble' she reminded him that he invariably became choked up whenever he read that same line – Johnson, too, knew a thing or two about Latin poetry. Clearly this is a poem capable of inspiring deeply personal reactions; only consider its innumerable musical settings down the ages. Hence – at last the point of this long preamble – when I am at times moved to write something *de profundis* I am often drawn to the outward form at least of the *Dies Irae*, with its extraordinarily succinct rhythmic trochaic scheme and rhyming stanzas. Almost by default the resulting lines assume the form of a prayer.

> *Luna mane lucens clare,*
> *gaudens Sole nunc micare,*
> *nequit umbra te uelare.*
>
> *Luna lucis Solis plena*
> *labens super me serena,*
> *neque tractat te catena,*
>
> *quae retractat me submissum*
> *ex Olympo nunc demissum,*
> *uinctum sine spe amissum.*

Luna lenis, me precatum
iuues scire meum fatum
terra non in caelis natum.

Metre: Rhythmic trochaic

Translation:

O morning Moon shining brightly, now delightfully sparkling with the Sun, no shadow can hide you. O Moon full of sunlight gliding serenely over me, no chain drags you, which now drags me back, thrown down from the heights, submissive, defeated, lost without hope. O gentle Moon, help me who addresses [you] to understand that my place is on the earth not in the heavens.

*   *   *

6 Cantilenae
uel
sententiae cottidianae frequenter repetendae

Mark writes: The Italian musical term *cantilena*, related to Latin *cantus*, indicates a smooth-flowing melodic line. But the Romans employed that same word to describe an oft-repeated refrain, like the chorus of the annoying pop song you heard on the radio this morning that you just can't get out of your head. Hence it was also used to describe a commonplace, a platitude. But such hackneyed aphorisms designed expressly for repetition have their place in philosophy, too: think of the Buddhist practice of reciting mantras as a way of fully absorbing their religion's tenets. Likewise, the ancient philosophical schools of Athens and Rome understood that reasoned argument alone is not sufficient: our brains need something more readily accessible and easy to remember if we are fully to internalise their teachings. Epicurus has his Principal Doctrines, Epictetus advocated regular recitation of Stoic teachings, and his *Enchiridion* ('Handbook') is a collection of just such stock phrases, tailor-made for frequent repetition by his students; his most devoted follower, Marcus Aurelius, filled his *Meditations* with similar self-admonitory precepts. (Curious readers could do worse than to acquire a copy of Pierre Hadot's *Philosophy as a Way of Life* [Blackwell, 1995], a lucid exposition of these and other practical aspects of ancient philosophy.) What follows are my attempt at casting some everyday animadversions on impatience, vanity, anger and the like, into easy-to-remember couplets addressed to myself in the hope that by writing them down then reciting them I will not only better be able to absorb the lesson, but also more easily call them to mind in times of need – and that's the real point: to make them simple enough to recall under duress. As well as being determinedly unoriginal in content, they make no claims to much poetical merit either. The English paraphrases capture their prosaic nature.

(1)

iam culpas alias animo patientius aequo
ferre tibi liceat, nec tolerare tuas.

> Be patient of people's faults, but not your own.

(2)

> *natura aduersa, rationeque mente neganti,*
> *ne capias uanas consilia atque uias.*

> Don't make plans that can't be realised.

(3)

> *non tibi non umquam circum te uoluitur orbis;*
> *uel te uel non te uoluitur orbis item.*

> You are not the centre of the universe.

(4)

> *est puerilis se flammare frequenter ad iram;*
> *sit se contentus tempore maior homo.*

> Anger is a sign of immaturity – grow up.

(5)

> *quod potes, hoc facias bene, fortiter atque libenter;*
> *nec te paeniteat quod nequit illud agi.*

> Do the best you can and don't worry about the rest.

(6)

> *res ipsae modo res, rerum modo motus inanis;*
> *mens solus regnumst imperiumque tuum.*

> Shit happens – you are only responsible for yourself.

Metre: Elegiacs

*   *   *

Non Credo

Mark writes: My own 'backwards' take on a *Credo*. The word *caduca* ("earthly things") is typically used pejoratively as a contrast to *aeterna*, the higher and the heavenly. But for me, that's just the wrong way round.

in nullosque deos, in nullaque numina credo,
inque caduca magis credere uiua uolo

Metre: Elegiacs

Translation: (paraphrase) I prefer to believe in this living world than invisible spirits in the sky.

*   *   *

Felix Iste

Mark writes: I was inspired to pen this small piece after a concert where, among other items, I heard a performance of a motet by Vivaldi (RV629), the text of which intrigued me as an example of an interesting rhythmic metre. The first stanza is:

> *Longe mala, umbrae, terrores,*
> *sors amara iniqua sors.*
> *Bella plagae irae furores*
> *tela et arma aeterna mors.*

I particularly liked the cadence *umbrae terrores ... irae furores*, which is a rhythmical Adonic. Note my 'homage' (i.e. blatant plagiarism) in the use of *mors ... sors*. *Felix Iste* describes the kind of happy-go-lucky type who seem able to float through life without a care in the world: an enviable state, surely, but one I have decidedly mixed feelings about.

> *felix iste, homo iucundus,*
> *quem oblita relinquit mors,*
> *semper mouet uentus secundus,*
> *semper spernit seuera sors.*
>
> *stultus iste, princeps stultorum,*
> *qui fortunae oblitus stat,*
> *mortis, sortis, uitae ludorum,*
> *qui fidelis se fatis dat.*

Metre: Rhythmic trochaic/iambic

Translation:

> That happy-go-lucky guy, whom forgetful death ignores, always with the wind at his back, never the victim of bad luck. That idiot, prince of idiots, forgetful of fortune, of death, of chance, of the tricks of life, who with blind trust gives himself to the fates.

*   *   *

Cupido Honoris Vana
(elegia modulata)

Mark writes: These are odd and decidedly un-classical elegiac couplets with Leonine rhymes in both the hexameter and pentameter – those in the pentameter forming repetitive, chorus-like refrains. I have laid out the poem below in half-lines to make it look (as well as read) more like a modern (or at least medieval) song lyric than a classical poem. Standard layout would be:

spes aspernatae, non acceptae nec amatae
atque meis dominis, atque meis animis ...

The layout below is an experiment in how such classical verse might be adapted to make it more suitable for musical setting. This and the following accentual poem *Fragilitas* form a pair on the same subject.

spes aspernatae,
non acceptae nec amatae
atque meis dominis
atque meis animis.

quare dic quaeso
noceatis me mihi laeso,
absque meo clipeo,
hostibus in cuneo?

solus languesco,
deceptus fraude tabesco,
in laqueis stupide,
carceribus cupide.

scriptis illectis
et consiliisque senectis,
dedecus accipio,
sordidus excipio.

nec me dementem,
necnon obtestor amentem:
mens iterum ualeat,
spes iterum redeat!

Metre: Leonine (rhyming) elegiacs

Translation: *The vain seeking after distinction*

O spurned hopes – neither agreeable to nor desired both by my masters and my heart – tell me, I beg, why do you still hurt me when I am injured, without my shield, with my enemies arrayed against me? Alone I languish, deceived by a trick I pine in bonds foolishly, in prison eagerly. With my writings unread and my plans grown weary, I take up the shame, base as I am I accept it. I solemnly declare that I am not mad nor yet insane: let my mind be well once more, once more let hope return!

*   *   *

Fragilitas

Mark writes: A companion piece to *Cupido Honoris Vana* above, this is non-quantitative, accentual verse expressly written to be sung. The rhyme scheme is eight-syllabled iambic – or 8pp according to Dag Norberg's notation (*An Introduction to the Study of Medieval Latin Versification*) – with each stanza rhyming in the pattern aabccb. Note the alliteration of every third line, in which every word begins with the same letter; also the verbs in lines 3 and 6 of the first stanza are in the first person (*sentio ... fugio*), lines 9 and 12 of the second stanza are in the second-person (*memineris ... aberis*), and lines 15 and 18 of the third stanza are in the third person (*debeat ... noceat*).

in mente mea fragilem
me esse et difficilem
semperque semper sentio.
e uanis nunc consiliis
et uacuis praesidiis
furtiuus furtim fugio.

dum recido ad nihilum
in egestate tui sum
me miserum memineris.
dum mentis in paludibus
et desum potestatibus
absurde absens aberis?

nunc repulso a domino,
confuso me in animo,
donare donum debeat.
qui plenus potestatis fit
non nimis gloriosus sit,
nec nemini non noceat.

Metre: Rythmic iambic

Translation: *My Fragile Mind*

Ever and anon my mind feels fragile and troubled. Now furtively thief-like I flee from vain plans and empty strongholds. Will you remember miserable me while I amount to nothing, in need of your presence? Will you be away foolishly while my mind is in the mire and I am powerless? Now that I have been rejected by my master, my spirit in disorder, let him bestow a gift. He who is made powerful, let him not be excessively proud, nor hurt anyone.

*   *   *

Plato Mi

Mark writes: Plato is my Cavalier King Charles Spaniel. When he was just a puppy he inspired the first Latin poem I ever wrote.

tu carissimus es caniculorum,
Plato mi, mihi callidissimusque:
tu stertens quoque semper impudenter
stratis, me gelido, cubare raptis
furtiue potes immemorque dormis.
si fortasse ruas uiam iocose
pellens papilionem in aere agentem,
tu tutus mihi, machinis uitatis,
reddas semper, et immemorque mortis.
felicissimus es caniculorum.

Metre: Hendecasyllables

Translation: *Dear Plato*

You are to me, my dear Plato, the dearest of little dogs[1], and the most cunning: stealthily having stolen the sheets you lie down, shamelessly always snoring, too, and while I am shivering, heedless you sleep. If perhaps playfully you should rush headlong into the road putting to flight a butterfly fluttering on the breeze, may you always come back safe to me, having avoided the cars[2], and heedless of death. You are the luckiest of little dogs.

     1. *caniculorum* – diminutive for comic effect
     2. *machinis* – as in Italian 'machina'

*   *   *

In Colle Concauo Ambulans

Mark writes: One of my early efforts, commemorating walks with the dog on Coombe Hill above Wendover in Buckinghamshire.

amoena moles, optimi loci palmam
dedi tibi, dum prata per tua errabam:
ubique palor cum caniculo, passim
cuniculosas ille per uias currens
comesque laetus. hic columna nunc sursum,
stilus superbus imminens super campis
quibus sonorum tinnule sonat templum.
renidet aestas: murmurat iocosa aura
per arboresque uepribus susurratue,
crescitue uentus aptus ad uolandumque
uentosa uela: subuolant simul corda,
cadit deorsum in stragulis agris cura.

Metre: Scazons ('Limping' iambics)

Translation: *Rambling on Coombe[1] Hill*

O delightful hill, to you I have awarded the prize of best place of all as I rove through your meadows: I wander everywhere with my little dog, while he capers here and there along rabbity paths, a happy companion. Now here arises the column[2], a proud monument overhanging the plain, in which the sonorous church[3] rings clangingly. Summer shines cheerfully: playful breezes murmur through the trees or whisper among the bushes, or a wind increases suitable for flying breeze-blown kites[4]: at the same time as our hearts fly up, worries tumble down into the patchwork fields.

> 1. *concauo* – Coombe is an old English word for hollow
> 2. *columna* – the Boer war memorial at the summit of Coombe Hill, commanding views across Aylesbury vale and Oxfordshire
> 3. *templum* – the church of St. Peter and St. Paul in Ellesborough
> 4. *uela* – did the Romans fly kites?

*   *   *

Benjamin Wallach

Benjamin Wallach attends the Montclair Kimberley Academy where he enthusiastically studies Latin and serves as the president of his school's chapter of the New Jersey Junior Classical League. Though a deep admirer of Roman history, culture, and literature, the work featured in *Vates* marks his first foray into the composition of Latin poetry.

Five Quincouplets

Benjamin writes: First exposed to quincouplets through Andreas Lovaniensis' two wonderful compositions in the Autumn 2013 issue (*Vates* #8), I found myself immediately enthralled with this elegantly humble poetic style. Indeed, I soon realized that the almost epigrammatic quality of a quincouplet requires the poet to be at his most lucid and precise, a difficult but greatly rewarding necessity. In my first quincouplet presented here, for instance, I seek to capture the passing mental image of a great marble statue vivaciously examining those who go by. Thematically, I hope to present a literary situation (i.e., this sentient statue) that muddies the waters of our crisp living/non-living binary–all in just five words. This extreme constraint demands extraordinary care in word selection, though the fluidity of the Latin language still allows for creative word patterns (e.g., the placement of the prefix *praeter* at the very beginning of a line). The most important choice of words, though, pertains to the quincouplet's title, which constitutes a full sixth of the poem's content. For this work, I chose the title *Marmor*, not only as a reference to the statue's marble composition, but also because of the word's internal consonance, mirroring the (a)biotic duality discussed above.

Marmor

statua saxi
praetereuntes aspicit uiuide.

Marble.
A statue made of stone spiritedly gazes at those who walk past.

Adipisci

algor auola
aestus aestatis appropinquet.

Arriving.
Fly off wintery coldness and let the summer warmth approach!

Clustra

nix negotiumque
arduis compescuntur muris.

Bulwarks.
Snow and pain are kept out by my lofty walls.

Disparita

elanguens arbos
me antiquior ciuitateue.

About to Vanish.
A slumping tree, far more ancient than either the nation or I.

Aquaticae

dictum naues
lacrimis alti cadere.

Watery.
It is said that ships sink with the tears of the sea.

Metre: Quincouplets

[*The Editor adds*: "The rules of a quincouplet, or quin, are simple. There are two lines, with two words on the first line and three words on the second. It need not have a title, but if it does, the title must consist of only one word. The title can be used for any purpose except as the first word of a sentence continued by the poem."]

*   *   *

Brad Walton

Brad Walton lives in Toronto. He did a BA in Classics and graduate work in Theology, which seems to have been a dreadful mistake. His study of Jonathan Edwards (*Jonathan Edwards, Religious Affections, and the Puritan Analysis of True Piety, Spiritual Sensation and Heart Religion*) was published in 2002. More recently an attempt at Menippean satire, *Peripedemi Periegesis*, was serialized in *Melissa*. His play, "The Dialogues of Leopold and Loeb" is being produced in Toronto in 2016. His day-job is in the University of Toronto Library. In his spare time he plays theorbo for the Toronto Continuo Collective, directed by Lucas Harris.

Ex Umbris

Brad writes: The poet is in a deep depression. He warns the reader not to expect "lumen". Yet a pun might supply it. The mental torpor of depression is not likely to yield anything so intellectually vigorous as an aphorism. Yet one might slip out, nevertheless. Maybe even two in one. This is a poem that promises nothing, and yet gives readers their money's worth.

> *haec, qua uersificor, superat caligine sedes*
> *illunem noctis faciem, demersa profundis*
> *oceani tenebris spissas tot combibit umbras*
> *ut fluat obscuro digitis depressa supellex.*
> *nox media obcaecat uultus et uoce Quiritum*
> *eloquitur. par sum minimis animantibus, imo*
> *quae repunt pelago, madidis aut foeda cauernae*
> *haerent parietibus suspensaque uertice cessant.*
> *heu, mens cassa, manus steriles, labor inritus. exspes*
> *carnificis gladium maneo; gradus occupat aures.*
> *quid petis, o lector? quaenam tibi dona poeta*
> *sopitusque malis atri nebulaque uolutus*
> *praebeat? elinguem faciunt aduersa disertum.*
> *inuenies hoc tam furuo, philomuse, decoram*
> *nec sententiolam, nitidum nec carmine lumen.*

Metre: Hexameters

Translation:

This place where I write exceeds in blackness the moonless figure of the night. Submerged in the deepest shadows of the ocean, it has absorbed so many dense shadows that the furniture, pressed with the fingers, drips with darkness. Midnight dims the faces of the inhabitants and speaks out in their voices. I am like the tiny animals that creep at the bottom of the sea, or cling, noisome, to the damp walls of a cave, or rest suspended from the ceiling. I have searched the darkness and no light has glistened for me in my misery. Alas, my mind is empty, my hands are barren, my labour is useless. I wait, hopeless, for the executioner's blow. His footsteps ring in my ears. Reader, what are you looking for? What gifts could a poet, stunned by adversity and enveloped in darkness, offer you? Affliction dumbfounds the eloquent. In this dark poem you will find, o lover of the arts, no gracious aphorism or rhetorical flourish.

*   *   *

After the Raid

Brad writes: I have been working on a story poem in hexameters set during World War I on the Western Front. In the following excerpt, a hand-picked group of soldiers from a British battalion has raided a German trench in retaliation for a similar attack. Alfred is a company officer and also the architect and commander of the raid. Walter is one of his sergeants. This raid is Alfred's first experience of close combat.

auia per deserta suis redeuntibus orta
militibus maesta et turbata silentia sensit
Alfredus. nunc hic sistit, nunc ille, uomitque
corpore deflexo. reducem saluere cateruam
plurima gratantes laeti iussere cohortes.
grex uictor presso resalutant corde sodales,
atque ubi rem fortes breuiter retulere, reductas
in caueas umbrasque suas plerique recedunt.
e paucis et adhuc tristi certamine laetis
haud tenui Brennus turbam, momenta, cruorem
enarrat studio, iuuenes tenet atque loquellis.
*   Alfredo, ut cessit properans ad tecta, biformis*
sanguinei ruit in mentem terroris imago.
cernit utrumque sua uigilem uirtute cadentem,
imprudentem alium sica praecordia caesus,
occiput atque alii ruptum liquidasque cerebro
uallorum tabulas. surgit prensaque matella
exonerat diris trepidantia uiscera formis.
*   Gualterus ora luto sparsus, thorace cruore*
fuscata, caueae subit atque aduertit aqualem.
auersis tum dux oculis adfatur amicum,
"cum dedimus, nos si dedimus, bone Gualtere, mortem,

169

in fusis dedimus facto certamine campis
eminus armati, nobis nec uictima pandit
se nisi uix claram longinqua ex arce figuram,
nec fuimus certi an nostra sit glande peremptus.
hactenus occulta tulimus solamina mente,
missile non nostrum uita spoliasse. propinquus
nunc tamen occidi. submissa uoce loquentem
audissem. uidi faciem cutis atque colores
et motus animi, qui perspicerentur ocellis,
ingeniumque liquens: mitis uigil alter, amoenis
et deditus somnis; audacior alter et acer.
istis me pepulit caesis breuis horror, et illic
actutum capiunt coeptis enata secundis
gaudia, quae incursum clademque tulere per omnem.
nunc paris occisi captum retinentia torquet.
conscia profusi semper mens arguit ultrix
sanguinis immeriti et sacro de crimine damnat.”
“patrasti facinus praeclarum,” ait optio, “magni
et ducis egisti partes.” Alfredus at illi,
“ipse mihi uideor facinus patrasse nefandum.”
Gaulterus auertit uultus et “quotlibet,” inquit,
“conficiat rigido generosa et fortia bello,
plurimus at miles sibi, cum iugulauerit, etsi
aggredientem hostem iussusque, homicida uidetur.
haec, domine, occulta est Martis res maxima, nullus
quam populo uates enuntiat: esse reuersus
quae secum ferat ad patriam duo uulnera miles,
hostis quod teneris inflixerit artubus, et quod
ipse suae caedendo animae, repetentia saepe
aeternis laceraturum praecordia probris.
flere senes uidi post multa decennia caedem.
non iugulare soles. proprium mandare tribuni,
sed mactare uiros caligae. nunc sanguine tincta
bellantis, ductor, inspexti pectora uulgi.”
Alfredo in mentem Brennus uenit. “ut reor,” inquit,
“sunt quibus occidisse placet.” “placet,” optio reddit,
“nonnullis, inter centum fortasse duobus,
qui faciunt caedem, caedem meminere libenter,
atque iterum occidisse petunt. plerique uirorum
sclopeti nocuum uix adducuntur ad usum.”

*   *   *

Metre: Hexameters

Translation:

Alfred perceived the gloomy and troubled silence that had emerged among his soldiers as they returned through the wilderness of No Man's Land. Now one man, then another halted, bent his body, and vomited. The troops hailed the returning company with a shower of congratulations. The victorious squadron returned the greeting with subdued spirits and, when they had given a brief account of the business, most withdrew into the dark recesses of their dugouts. Among the few still elated from the grisly combat, Brian described with no little enthusiasm the chaos, the manoeuvres and the bloodshed, and held the youngsters spell-bound with his account.

As soon as Alfred had made a swift return to his quarters, a double image of blood-bespattered horror rushed into his mind. He saw both sentries falling in the midst of their own bravery, one, taken by surprise, cut down by a bayonette to the chest, the other, the back of his head blown out and the walls of the trench streaming with his brains. Alfred jumped up, seized the bed pan and emptied his stomach, which churned with the terrible memories.

Walter, his face spattered with mud and his jacket dark with gore, entered the dug-out and noticed the basin. His officer, having turned his eyes away, addressed him as a friend. "When we killed (if, Walter, it was we who killed), we did so armed at a distance, in an engagement set on a sprawling battlefield. The victim did not present himself except as a distant figure on a far-off rampart. Moreover, we were never certain whether he had been killed by our bullet. Until now we could take this consolation in the secrecy of our thoughts, that it was not our weapon that had taken life. But now I have killed at close range. I could have heard one speaking in a whisper. I saw their faces, the complexion of their skin, whatever feelings could be seen in the eyes, and their personalities as clear as crystal. One sentry was mild and given to pleasant reveries. The other was bolder and fiercer. Their deaths struck me with a brief horror, and immediately, in reaction to our initial success, an elation came over me and carried me through the entire slaughter. Now the memory of that slain pair clutches and tortures me. My guily mind constantly denounces me for spilling innocent blood and condemns me of an accursed crime."

"It was a fine achievement for you. You played your part as a great leader."

"I feel as though I have committed a terrible outrage."

Walter turned his face away and said, "No matter how many fine, brave deeds a soldier carries out in the rigours of war, often, when he has killed an enemy, even an attacking one and under orders, he feels that he is a murderer. This, sir, is the deepest secret of war, which no poet ever tells the people: there are two wounds that a soldier carries home to his country. One is the wound that the enemy has inflicted on his vulnerable body, and the other is that which he has inflicted on himself by killing. This shreds his remembering heart with perpetual reproaches. I have seen old men weep over a killing done decades before. You are not used to killing. An officer's job is to command. Killing is the job of the rank and file. Now, sir, you have seen into a common soldier's blood-stained heart."

Brian came into Alfred's thoughts. "I suppose," he said, "that there are some people who like to kill."

His sergeant replied, "Perhaps two in every hundred like to kill, gladly remember having killed, and seek to kill again. Most men can hardly be persuaded to fire a shot in anger."

*   *   *

171

Three Drinking Songs

Brad writes: I spent much of one summer writing drinking songs, generally at my local pub. Most of the regulars there are older gentleman of retirement age. I was thinking of them, obviously, when I wrote *Anacreonticum Senile* and *Diutius Vivere*. *Bibamus, Sodales* is intended for anyone of drinking age. Incidentally, it was written before the European fiscal crisis burst on the world. Otherwise that would certainly have been mentioned in my catalogue of current catastrophes.

(1) Anacreonticvm Senile

premit aetas, ueterani
  uicium dolumque uitae.
abit Auster iuuenilis,
  Boreas adit senilis,
cineres et tenebrosum
  ferimur leues in orbem.
neque amamus uelut amplum
  iuuenes amant theatrum
speciosa ubi furibundum
  peragit facinora saeclum.
fere cunctis uariemus
  pretiis ut aestimandis,
tamen inter legiones
  iuuenum senumque constat
Dionysum genialis
  caput esse suauitatis,
et alentem celebrandum
  Cererem dedisse donum.
glacialis domat acrem
  cereuisia solis aestum
cumulatque societatem
  citat et dicacitatem;
iuuenes soluit honesti
  ualidis obicibus usus,
moderamine nimio leuat
  animos diu repressos;
uetulis excutit umbras
  animis supermeantes,
epularum et superarum
  bibulis dat arrhabonem.

Metre: alternating ionic dimeters and anacreontics

Translation: *Old Person's Drinking Song*

Age weighs on us, veterans of life's ups, downs, and delusions. The south wind of youth departs, the north wind of old age approaches, and we are being borne like weightless ashes into the world of darkness. We are not so enamoured, as are the young, of the vast theatre where the mad world plays out its glamorous misdeeds. Though we differ in our evaluation of almost everything, still the cohorts of the young and old agree that Dionysus is the source of delightful sweetness, and that kindly Ceres has given us a gift to be celebrated. Frosty beer overcomes the sharp heat of the sun, increases comraderie and inspires wit. It releases young people from the strong constraints of respectable propriety; it relieves spirits long repressed by excessive control. It shakes off the shadows creeping over the souls of the old, and gives to them as they drink a foretaste of the parties in heaven.

*   *   *

(2) *Bibamus, Sodales*

bibamus, sodales, neque obstent inanes
crumenae facetis et doctis loquelis,
animis uel benignis et amicis catenis,
uel curis in horas aliquot derelictis.
ahenum in camino, planetes calescit.
glacialis polorum uetustas liquescit
et ursus niuosus spoliatur scabello.
se tollens profundum frequentes in oras
fugat nationes penatibus aquosis.
palatia Tonantis modo ardent, modo algent.
feroces procellae tellurem flagellant
meatusque flumina tumentia redundant
et fundos et hortos et aedes inundant.
patescit caelestem fuligo per orbem,
petroleum coinquinat et agros et aequor.
purgaminis Olympi sub aruis humantur
natant et marini per undas barathri.
lymphis profluentes arescunt regiones,
et inter sitientes Mauors intumescit
pro parcis mundarum fluentis aquarum
locupletes crebrescunt, egentes abundant,
mediocri rarescunt thesauro beati.
habent cuncta pauci, nihil multitudo.
dum dites aceruant, plebei uix ullum

parant quaestuosum retinent uel laborem.
rerum publicarum rationes turbatae,
Columbia suis intumescit uenenis.
iacet collocatae uorago monetae,
et nobis misellae per annos corrasae
opes in trapeza seruatae macrescunt.
alimur spe uiriles ut alamur seniles,
inopem praeuidemus tamen omnes senectam.

Metre: Bacchiac tetrameters

Translation: *Friends, Let Us Drink*

Friends, let us drink, and do not let empty wallets stand in the way of witty and well-informed banter, or of kindly spirits and the bonds of friendship, or of abandoning care for a few hours. The planet warms like a pot on a stove. The primordial ice caps are melting and the polar bear is robbed of his footstool. The sea, rising against the crowded coastlines, chases peoples away from their flooded homes. The sky blazes one moment and freezes the next. Fierce storms whip the land, and the swollen rivers overflow their channels to inundate farms, gardens, and houses. Soot spreads through the celestial sphere. Oil pollutes land and sea. Mountains of garbage are buried underground, or float over the waves of the oceanic abyss. Water-rich countries go dry and war flares up among the thirsty for scant streams of clean water. The wealthy increase. Paupers abound. The middle class grows scarce. A few have everything. Many have nothing. While the rich heap up their wealth, the poor can hardly get or keep a job The balance sheets of the State are a mess. America swells with its own toxins. The vortex of investment is in ruins, and our pittance, scraped together over the years and deposited in the bank, wastes away. As adults we feed on the hope that we will be fed in our dotage, yet we all anticipate an impoverished old age.

*　　　*　　　*

(3) Diutius Viuere

Aurora, rubens diua, perennis et puella,
Tithonum adamat Cypride roscida nitentem,
uerno ualidum sanguine ferreisque neruis,
hominem tamen, ac legibus insitis caducum.
a patre deum uiuificis rogat uenustae
in perpetuum deliciae fruantur auris.
sed mente leui diua misella, obliuiosa
tantum rogat ut morte maritus eximatur,
non ut careat tempore temporisque damnis.
ergo, socii, fundite Bacchicos liquores,
tristes animos soluite rebus inuenustis
praesentibus et praeteritis et adfuturis.

174

iam iam, comites, huic radians patrona saeclo,
artis medicae lux facit ut noui recente
Pallantiadis numine candidae mariti
abiecta putris fata supersimus salutis,
macie domito corpore, mente dissoluta,
dum clara dii tela diutius tuentes
nos liuor edat Ditem adeuntium profundo
nondum senio debilium, quibus superstes
et adhuc aliquid corporei uigoris exstat,
necnon aliquid sospitis integraeque mentis.

Metre: Sotadeans

Translation: *Living too Long*

Aurora, rubicund goddess and perennial girl, falls for Tithonus, sparkling with dewy Venus, strong in the spring-time of his vigour and iron muscles, but yet a human being, and doomed by his natural condition to perish. From the the father of the gods she asks that her delightful darling enjoy the life-giving air forever. But the poor, dizzy, forgetful goddess only asks that her husband be exempt from death, not from time or the damages of time. So, friends, pour out the liquors of Dionysus. Release your sad minds from present, past and future unpleasantness. Nowadays, comrades, nowadays the luminous art of medicine, the patroness shining on this age, sees to it that we, the new husbands of a dawn bright with fresh divinity, survive the pitiful death of our withered health, our bodies wasted away, our minds dissolved, until beholding the bright shafts of day too long, we envy those who approach death not yet disabled with extreme old age, for whom there yet survives something of corporeal vigour and something of a sound, unimpaired mind.

*   *   *

Three Sea Poems

Brad writes: These three poems are all related, however loosely, to the sea. This is a good theme in Latin since the language has so many synonyms for sea: *mare, aequor, altum, profundum, pontus, fretum, salum, gurges, undae, pelagus, marmor, oceanus, Neptunus, Thetis, Nereus, Tethys.* In the last poem, *Piscatores*, the sea referred to is, of course, the Sea of Galilee. I had to resist the temptation of referring to it as *oceanus*, in spite of the metrical convenience of that word. I thought it probably too small to pass convincingly as an 'ocean'.

(1) Naufragi Formosi

aequoreo demersus Apolline
quisque suis in litoribus iacet
naufragus indomitisque soporibus
restituit quae robora sorbuit

immensum pelagus. ceruicibus
sub lepidis deiecta cubilia
e tenui sabulone, rudentibus,
retibus, euersae trabibus ratis,
sole dealbatis ramalibus,
couraliis ornata rubentibus,
taeniolis algae, lolligine,
electro, stella, testudine.
rore maris trepidi manat coma.
sparsa cutis, cilium, mollis gena,
labra procacia marmoreo sale.
litoreus subter scapulis calor,
et porrecta gracillima brachia
formoso maris in purgamine.

Metre: Dactylic tetrameter

Translation: *The Beautiful Castaways*

Immersed in the ocean sun light, each shipwrecked sailor lies on his beach and with irresistible sleep restores the strength swallowed by the vast sea. Cast beneath their graceful necks are beds of fine stones, ropes, nets, the timbers of their sunken ship, branches bleached by the sun, (beds) adorned with red corals, ribbons of seaweed, cuttle-fish, amber, starfish, tortoise shell. Their hair drips with the dew of the unquiet sea. Their skin, eyelids, soft cheeks, wanton lips are sprinkled with sea salt. Beneath their shoulder blades is the warmth of the beach, and their slender arms are stretched over the beautiful refuse of the sea.

*   *   *

(2) Neptunus Iuuenis

olim caeruleo fuit
Neptuno nitor aureus,
pingui caesarie caput,
nigritudo supercili,
fulgentes oculi nouis
optatis et amoribus,
purae mollities cutis,
imberbisque rubor genae,
labri puniceus tumor,
ceruix lactea, turgidae
pectoris calyces rosae,
neruorum teretum rigor,
planum uentris aheneum,

contractique uenustulus
et lentus medii sinus.
nec raro iuuenis deus,
fratre uictus Olympico,
maerens Palladis Atticam,
spretus frugifera dea,
prolixos cilii pilos
largis imbuit imbribus
et sparsit nitido rudem
se dolens faciem uitro.

Metre: Glyconics

Translation: *Young Neptune*

Once blue Neptune had a golden sheen, a head of thick hair, black eyebrows, eyes blazing with new desires and passions, soft, unblemished skin and a red flush on his beardless cheeks, a purple fullness to his lips, a white neck, nipples like swelling roses, the firmness of well-turned muscles, a bronze flatness to his stomach, and a graceful and supple curve to his slender waist. It was not unusual for the young god, defeated by his Olympian brother, lamenting Attica possessed by Minerva, scorned by the fruit bearing goddess, to soak his long eye lashes with plentiful showers and, grieving for himself, to sprinkle his callow face with sparkling glass.

*   *   *

(3) *Piscatores*

fulget lineus aether.
flagrant aequoris undae.
celso sidere cocta
torret litus harena.
iuxta somniculosum
bini marmor ephebi,
par praestabile, fratres
et piscator uterque,
duplex fulmen, acuto
nudae lumine formae
sciti retia curant.
consorbinus in oram
prodit datque salutem.
neuter perspicit ille
quis sit quidque loquatur,

ast uterque suopte
frater more calescit:
maior dicta perardet,
dicentem minor ipsum.

Metre: Pherecrateans

Translation: *Fishermen*

The flax-blue sky shimmers, the waves of the sea blaze, the beach burns with sand baked by the noon-day sun. By the drowsy sea two young brothers, an exceptional pair and both fishermen, a double thunderbolt, skilfully mend their nets in the keen lustre of their naked beauty. Their cousin appears on the shore and greets them. Neither fully understands who he is and what he is saying, but each brother in his own way grows hot: the older is afire for his words, the younger for the speaker himself.

*   *   *

Euitans Euitatus

(a Pub Poem)

Brad writes: I think you might call this a slice-of-life poem, in the tradition of Catullus 10. It is based on an experience at my neighbourhood pub. It is written in Phalaecian hendecasyllables, but without the elegant regularities usually observed by later poets, such as Martial and Statius. These just don't seem to me appropriate in a tipsy atmosphere. Perhaps I should add that, since writing this poem, the gentleman and I have become good friends and have found enough common interests to furnish topics of conversation, though classical literature isn't one of them.

est uir qui celebrat meam popinam
nequaquam rudis aut ineptus, illis,
quae gratos bibulis solent amicis
sermones agitare, disciplinis
(hocceio, pedifollio, palaestra,
harpasto, patinatione) doctus,
hactenusque reconditis nouarum
tinctus munditiis scientiarum, ut
potores adeat seueriores.
fertur praeterea esse luculentus
re mathematica peritus, olim
qui nummaria cum negotia obiret,
tantis quaestibus auxerit crumenam
ut quamuis iuuenis pedem referret
iam praediues in otium senile.
turbatus dubio tamen furore

indefessus inambulat taberna;
secum mussitat et sibi iocatur,
cacchinans salit et salit solutus,
iactans brachia seque agens in orbes,
quaerens sollicitus quibus perennes
aspergat pluuias suae loquelae,
nec, donec parat hostiam, quiescit.
sed neglexerat usque segregatum
me cum Castaliis in angulo, dum
potores coluit facetiores.
at nuper, solitis, quibus fauebat,
cum caupona bibentibus uacaret,
hic furore magis magisque motus,
in me lumina coniicit. sed aures
contritas metuens mihique uires
ablatas animae superfluente
lymphatae fluuio loquacitatis,
contractis humeris, meum in libellum
demitto caput et recondo ocellos.
frustra! "quid legis?" audio rogari.
sic respondeo ut ille terreatur,
"nonnihil Senecae tragoediarum."
felix consilium satis superque.
nam retro saliens "eho!" profatur.
se statim recipit, fero per ora
contemptu studiique peruetusti
emicante uirique inelegantis.
"me quidni meritum putat," requiro,
"quocum naufragus ille colloquatur?"
iratus sedeo, dolens repulsam,
quadam spe latitante destitutus.

Metre: Hendecasyllables.

Translation:

The Avoider Avoided: There is a man who frequents my pub, by no means uncultivated or absurd, well-informed on subjects usually of interest to drinking companions (hockey, soccer, gymnastics, rugby, skating), and sufficiently familiar with the stylishly intriguing aspects of recent science to apporach the more serious-minded drinkers. Moreover it's said that he is a brilliant mathematician, who had made so much money working in finance that he retired very well-off while still a young man. However, he paces the pub incessantly, unsettled by some indeterminate lunacy. He mutters and jokes to himself, laughs, jumps up and down uninhibitedly, gesticulating, turning himself in circles, agitatedly looking for someone to drench with the interminable downpour of his chatter, and can't calm down until he has found a victim. But he had always ignored me, secluded as I was in a corner with my literary pursuits, while he cultiviated the more elegant drinkers. Recently, however, when the pub was deserted of his usual favourite imbibers, increasingly agitated by his madness, he cast his eyes on me. I, afraid of having my ears worn out and my vital energy swept away by an inundating flood of his looney loquacity, hunched my shoulders, dropped my head and buried my eyes in my book. In vain. I hear the question, "What are you reading?" I replied in a manner to discourage him, "Something from Seneca's tragedies." My strategy worked – and all too well. With a backward jump he exclaimed, "Oh ho!" He beat an immediate retreat, a fierce disdain flashing over his face for an antiquated study and a complete nerd. I ask, "Why does that wreck of a man think me not worth talking to?" I sit there resentfully, smarting at the rejection, disappointed of some lurking hope.

*   *   *

Iter Nauticum

(A polymetric poem)

Brad writes: This is an experiment at writing a poem which shifts from one metre to another. I have observed *synaphea* throughout, though I am not sure it was entirely necessary, except in the anapestic bit. The final section recalls those innumberable photographs, taken in the late nineteenth and early twentieth centuries, of sailors dancing with each other on a boat deck, there being no women available.

iam tergum trepidat maris.
rauco gutture subdolae
replent flamina gauiae,
dum solis tremulum iubar
frangunt pectore candido
pendentes super undas.
hoc pelagus scatet omnis originis
aequoreis beluis: acipensere,
mugile, pistrice, murice, sidere,
locusta, polypo, testudine,
balaena, thynno, torpedine,
delphinis et hirudinibus.
secat altum cita nauis
patulumque radit aequor.
salis aurae redolentes
faciem comasque uerrunt.
tenui tollitur aestus
nebula ruente prora,

180

sociatur pluuiali
croceo phaselus arcu.
pedibus nudis tabulata premunt
nautae properi. tremulos funes
alii laxant, alii intendunt.
caua uela trahunt. malos superant
et ab aeria quaerunt specula
scopulos, syrtes, dubios latices.
celeramus per hiatus
ad Apollinem cadentem.
ferus aster in ocellos
iacit ultimas sagittas.
sub aquas numine merso
petimus uagas tenebras.
mare subter micat ater,
super ater alget axis.
nauta sub arcturo choreas agit,
expromptis citharis et carmine,
profuso Bromio et Cerealibus.
est gena iuncta genae, manui manus,
et medium leuiter corpus tenet
indiga palma nouae Cythereidos.
hic clausis oculis sui
saltat melliculi memor.
hic gaudens tenera premit
praesens delicium manu.
hic liuore dolens graui
diro saeuit amore.

Metres:

- Lines 1-5: glyconics
- 6: pherectratean
- 7-11: dactylic tetrameter
- 12: dactylic tetrameter catalectic
- 13-20: alternating ionic dimeter and anacreontics
- 21-26: anapestic dimeter
- 27- 34: alternating ionic dimeter and anacreontics
- 35-40: dacylic tetrameter
- 41-45: glyconics
- 46: pherecratean.

Translation: *Sea Journey*:

Now the spine of the sea shivers. The crafty sea-gulls fill the wind with their strident cries while they break the shimmering sun beams against their white breasts, hovering over the waves. The ocean teems with marine creatures of every kind: sturgeon, mullets, sharks, murex, star fish, lobster, octopus, turtles, whales, tuna, sting rays, dolphins and leeches. The swift craft cuts the deep and skims over the surface of the sea. Salty breezes sweep one's face and hair. The swell is lifted into a fine mist by the speeding prow. The vessel is accompanied by a saffron rainbow. The busy sailors press the deck with their bare feet. Some relax the quivering ropes, others pull them tight. They draw in the billowing sails. They climb to the top of the masts to spot the rocks, shoals and doubtful waters from the crow's nest. We speed over the ocean chasm toward the west. The fierce sun fires his last rays into our eyes. With the god sunk beneath the water we head for the shifting darkness. Beneath us the black sea sparkles. Above us the black pole grows cold. Under Arcturus the sailors dance, having broken out the guitars and the songs, having poured out the wine and beer. A cheek is pressed to a cheek, a hand to a hand, and a palm aching for fresh romance lightly holds a waist. One dances with eyes closed, remembering his sweet heart. One ecstatically presses his love in person with his fond hand. One, smarting with oppressive jealousy simmers with ominous passion.

*   *   *

Cogitans Libouuum

Brad writes: This is an attempt to translate a poem by Tu Fu (712-770 c.e.), into Latin. The original is composed of eight lines of five syllables each, a caesura after the second syllable of each line, and the same rhyme throughout, occurring on alternate lines. All I have tried to imitate of the original is its concentrated expression. I offer three translations: A literal one of the Latin, a literal and an expanded one of the original (by David Hawkes, *A Little Primer of Tu Fu*, Oxford, 1967).

> *tellus gelascit ultima.*
> *mihi quid, magister, diceres?*
> *quando anser aduolauerit?*
> *autumnus auget flumina.*
> *odit beatum Cynthius.*
> *scopulis morantur daemones.*
> *laesis locutus manibus,*
> *demitte carmen fluctibus.*

Metre: Iambic dimeter

Translation 1:

THINKING OF LI PO

The limit of the world ices over.
What would you say to me, teacher?
When will the goose fly this way?
Autumn swells the rivers.

Apollo hates a happy man.
The daemons are waiting on the cliffs.
Speak to the injured ghost
and drop a poem into the current.

Translation 2: Literal translation of the Chinese:

THINKING OF LI PO FROM THE ENDS OF THE EARTH

Cold wind rises world's end
Gentleman's ideas like what
Wild-goose what-time arrive
Rivers-lakes autumn-water much
Literature hates destiny-successful
Mountain demons rejoice people passing
Ought with wronged-ghost talk
Drop poem present Mi-lo.

Translation 3: Interpreted translation of the Chinese:

THOUGHTS OF LI PO FROM THE WORLD'S END

Here at the world's end the cold winds are beginning to blow. What
message have you for me, my master? When will the poor wandering
goose arrive? The rivers and lakes are swollen with autumn's waters.
Art detests a too successful life; and the hungry goblins await you with
welcoming jaws. You had better have a word with the ghost of that other
wronged poet. Drop some verses into the Mi-lo as an offering to him.

*   *   *

Appendix: Some Advice for Beginners

From the pages of Vates*, the editor's musings on a few areas of interest to both prospective and current poets*

(1) Start with Trochees

Trochaic verse, an extremely popular form in medieval Latin, is a great place to begin composing in Latin. It has an easy-to-understand rhythm and uses rhyming line endings, hence closely resembles English vernacular poetry. Unlike the quantitative verse of the classical Roman poets, this is all about word **stress**.

A *trochee* is a two-beat metrical 'foot' with the stress accent falling on the first beat (so, "<u>dum</u>-de, <u>dum</u>-de, <u>dum</u>-de, <u>dum</u>-de"). Constrast with an *iamb*, in which the stress falls on the second beat. Since Latin generally dispenses with the particles we rely on so much in English ('a', 'the' etc.) it tends to fall more naturally into a trochaic rhythm. In English, by contrast, an iambic rhythm is more common, e.g. the classic iambic pentameter of Shakespeare: "a <u>horse</u>, a <u>horse</u>, my <u>king</u>dom <u>for</u> a <u>horse</u>" ("di-dum, di-dum, di-dum" etc.).

Perhaps the best and most famous example of Latin trochaic verse is the magnificent *Dies Irae* of the Requiem Sequence. Each highly characteristic stanza consists of three rhyming lines of four trochaic feet each (the <u>underlined</u> syllables are stressed):

> <u>di</u>es <u>i</u>rae, <u>di</u>es <u>il</u>la
> <u>sol</u>vet <u>sae</u>clum <u>in</u> fa<u>vil</u>la
> <u>tes</u>te <u>Da</u>vid <u>cum</u> Si<u>byl</u>la

> ["Day of wrath, that day / When the world will dissolve into ashes / As predicted by David and the Sibyll."]

For anyone who has wrestled with the intricacies of quantitative verse it will be a relief to notice first of all that word stress is not subject to the same rules as syllable weight. So, the final *–es* and *–ae* of *Dies irae* are unstressed, though they would both count as 'heavy' syllables in quantitative verse. (The word *dies* actually scans as an iamb in quantitative verse, but here it is a trochee). Nor does the syllable ending the word *solvet* become stressed, despite being followed by another consonant beginning the next word *saeclum*. Nor, for that matter, is the final syllable of *saeclum* elided even though it ends in an 'm' and is followed by a word beginning with a vowel. Here word stress is king.

You might notice a preponderance of two-syllabled words. There's a good reason for that. In a typical two-syllable Latin word the stress accent falls on the first syllable. Hence <u>Di</u>es <u>i</u>rae, <u>di</u>es <u>il</u>la. So the simplest way to create a trochaic line is to stick with two-syllabled words. Fortunately, many basic Latin nouns and verbs are just such words – making this a verse form that even students with only a rudimentary vocabulary can use very early on in their Latin studies. It's a fun way for teachers to encourage Latin composition: give students a list of words they already know and see what they can create.

Things get even more interesting if you use three-syllable words. These are stressed on their second syllable if it has a long vowel or is followed by two consonants. So, in the *Dies irae* above we have stress accents on the second syllable of *favilla* and *Sibylla*. Hence, too, *Fortuna* in the opening of the famous *Carmina Burana*:

> *O Fortuna,*
> *velut luna*

["O Fortune, like the moon ..."]

Observe how the opening 'O' is necessary to establish the trochaic rhythm. The poet provides variety in the next few lines:

> *statu variabilis*
> *semper crescis*
> *aut decrescis*
> *vita detestabilis*

["changeable in state, you are always waxing or waning, detestable life"]

Here we have straightforward two-foot trochees (*semper crescis ... aut decrescis*) alternating with longer lines that have an extra syllable at the end (or rather, are missing a final syllable to complete an additional foot) – *statu variabilis ... vita detestabilis* – both of which consist of three-and-a-half feet. Such 'hanging' lines are technically known as *catalectic*. Note also how those four lines rhyme in the pattern A B B A.

Thanks to the inflected endings of Latin nouns and adjectives, such rhymes are relatively easy to achieve. Latin verb participles are especially helpful. Here's how the poet of the *Dies Irae* (probably Thomas of Celano, 1190-1260) uses future participles in the second stanza:

> *quantus tremor est futurus*
> *quando iudex est venturus*
> *cuncta stricte discussurus.*

["What dread there will be / When the Judge shall come / To judge all things severely."]

And he varies the same idea a little later on:

> *quid sum miser tunc dicturus,*
> *quem patronum rogaturus,*
> *cum vix iustus sit securus?*

["What then am I, wretch, to say / What advocate am I to ask to defend me / When the just may hardly be secure?"]

One final example – perfect participles this time. The terrifying fate awaiting the damned described in a brilliant ablative absolute clause. These are the lines so memorably discussed in the movie *Amadeus*, as the dying Mozart asks Salieri to transcribe his immortal musical setting:

> *confutatis maledictis*
> *flammis acribus addictis,*
> *voca me cum benedictis.*

185

["When the damned have been confounded / And sacrificed to the bitter flames / Call me with the blessed."]

Powerful stuff, powerfully conveyed. Notice particularly the double-stresses in the four-syllabed _confutatis maledictis_ ... _benedictis_.

So, if you are a little put off by the complexities of classical quantity, or even if you want to add some spice to your Latin versifying, try composing a few trochaic lines. If you play around with the rhythm and rhyme (couplets, triplets, catalectic lines, alternating rhymes etc. etc.) you can create remarkable effects using even a basic vocabulary.

* * *

(2) Vowels vs. Syllables

A great source of potential confusion for those who first encounter quantitative Latin verse is the distinction between vowel **length** and syllable **quantity**, which is all too often blurred or ignored in textbooks, especially older ones. We are told cavalierly of long and short syllables, and vowels that mysteriously become 'long by position', when what is actually meant is heavy and light syllables (their **quantity**) as distinct from the natural (and unvarying) **length** of vowels.

Vowel length is a matter of pronunciation. Vowels have a certain fixed length, as in the 'o' of 'dog' (short vowel) or the 'o' of 'bone' (long vowel). A short vowel is pronounced as a short vowel wherever it is placed in a line of quantitative verse. It never magically becomes long 'by position'.

Quantity on the other hand is a matter of syllable structure. Heavy syllables are those containing long vowels or ones that are 'closed' by a consonant followed immediately by a new syllable that begins with another consonant (with some exceptions). These heavy syllables were thought of as taking longer to pronounce and therefore tended to receive more stress when spoken. Syllables are therefore said to have **weight**. As W.S. Allen noted as long ago as 1965 in his definitive study of Latin pronunciation, _Vox Latina_:

> 'As length is a property of vowels, quantity is a property of syllables; and although there are connexions between length and quantity in Latin, the two properties are to be clearly distinguished ... the reader should be warned that even in some current standard works there is considerable confusion between syllabic quantity and vowel length – a confusion for which the Greek grammarians are ultimately responsible.' [Chapter 6]

That confusion persists even today. David J. Califf's _Latin Meter and Verse Composition_ (Anthem Press, 2002), for example, talks of both long and short vowels as well as long and short syllables. In his rules for determining the quantity of syllables Califf states, 'A vowel followed by two consonants or a double consonant ... is generally long'; but immediately after, 'The final syllable of a word ending in a vowel and a single consonant is lengthened if the next word begins with a consonant'; then, 'But a short open vowel at the end of a word is generally not lengthened ...' [Section II, p.6]

But vowels are not lengthened – rather, it is the syllable weight that changes. A short vowel remains short, even if followed by two consonants.

- Vowels have <u>length</u> – long or short – which is a matter of pronunciation and does not change, regardless of position in a line of verse
- Syllables have <u>quantity</u> – heavy or light – and it is the specific pattern of syllables, determined by various rules, in a line of verse that defines the metre.

*   *   *

(3) Stress vs. Ictus

Word *stress* is simply the result of natural pronunciation – the syllable where the most emphasis is placed when it is spoken. *Ictus* on the other hand is the technical term for the underlying rhythm, or the places where the 'beat' falls in a line. In English and other modern vernacular verse, these two things tend to coincide, as we generally (but not always) place the naturally stressed syllable on the 'beat' of the verse, as in a typical iambic pentameter: 'A **horse**, a **horse**, my **king**-dom **for** a **horse**.'

But things are a little different in classical Latin verse. The tension between the syllable-based metrical pattern of a line (with its *ictus*) and the rhythm of natural word stress informs much quantitative verse, especially so in the classic hexameter. Take, for example, the first line of the *Aeneid*. As written below, the top numbers are the six metrical feet; the second line represents the syllabic pattern of the hexameter line (dactyls and trochees); then finally the words with long vowels marked by a macron:

```
1       2       3    4     5       6
⁻ ˘ ˘ | ⁻ ˘ ˘ | ⁻ ⁻ | ⁻ | ⁻ ˘ ˘ | ⁻ ⁻
arma uirumque canō, Trōiae quī prīmus ab ōrīs,
```

Notice how the word stress of *uirum* (naturally pronounced with the stress on the first syllable) is shifted to the second syllable by the addition of –*que*, i.e. the second syllable now becomes heavy and so carries the word stress. But note the vowel 'u' is <u>not</u> therefore pronounced as a long vowel.

At the beginning of a hexameter line stress and *ictus* must coincide (since the hexameter always begins on a heavy syllable), but elsewhere matters are more at the poet's discretion. In the middle of the line rhythmic pulse (*ictus*) and word stress can and frequently do fall out of synch. This is what musicians call syncopation, and just as in a good jazz tune it's all about playing 'off the beat'. Here is where the mid-line *caesura* (or break) comes into its own: by forcing a word to end in the middle of (usually) the third foot, the *caesura* has the effect of forcing the rhythm and word stress apart. Typically, however, this tension is resolved in the final two feet, as metrical rhythm and the stress accent at last come together in an audibly satisfying cadence (again, the parallel with music is clear). This final cadence is known as an Adonic – a dactyl followed by a spondee (or a trochee – the final syllable regarded as 'heavy'). In English the rhythm and stress are as in the phrase 'strawberry jam-jar', *dum-diddy dum-dum*.

Let's take once again that line from the *Aeneid* as our example, this time with the word stress made explicit in bold:

```
1        2        3    4      5        6
– ⌣ ⌣ | – ⌣  ⌣ | – – | –  ⌣ ⌣ | –  ⌣  ⌣ | – –
```
arma vi**rum**que **ca**nō, **Trō**iae **quī prī**mus ab **ō**rīs

Here, word stress and accent are 'syncopated' or out of synch in feet 2, 3 and 4. Because the stress accent of any two-syllable word falls on the first syllable, whether it is heavy or light, *cano* is stressed on its first syllable (even though the final 'o' is a long vowel making the second syllable heavy). Notice that the *caesura* after the word *cano* in the middle of the third foot makes that stressed first syllable fall 'off the beat' at the end of the second foot and a new word – *Troiae* – now has to begin on the 'offbeat' of the third. Notice too that the metre would permit the poet to swap the words *Troiae* and *qui* around – *qui Troiae* scans equally well – but if he had done so *Troiae* would have occupied the fourth foot all on its own, the stress-accent coinciding with the beat, something he presumably wanted to avoid. The line concludes with that resonant dactyl-spondee 'strawberry jam-jar': **prī** -mus ab | **ōr** - īs

Classical Latin verse doesn't rhyme, so this Adonic cadence provides readers/listeners with an audible signal that we have reached the end of the line. Most hexameters will conform to this pattern, which is typically achieved by ending with either a three-syllabled (stress on the second syllable) or a two-syllabled (stress on the first syllable) word, both of which can be seen in the opening of Lucretius' *De Rerum Natura*:

> *Aeneadum genetrix, hominum diuomque uoluptas,*
> *alma Venus, caeli subter labentia signa*   (*DRN*, I.1-2i)

Where the stress-accents and *ictus* fall:

```
5             6
| – ⌣  ⌣  | –    –
```
(diu-) | **om**que uol- |-**up** - tas

(lab-) | **en**tia | **sig** - na

Notice the addition of *-que* turns *diuom* (an archaic genitive plural) into a three-syllabled word and so shifts the stress to the second syllable (just as with Virgil's *uirumque*). But Lucretius being Lucretius, his work is chock full of (by later Augustan standards anyway) exceptional usages such as big pentasyllabic endings that fill both fifth and sixth feet – e.g. **com**posi**tu**ras, **ex**or**er**entur, **sim**plici**ta**te – or monosyllables for the final foot like *quae sunt, per se, ab re*. He is also happy to finish a line with such things as *quae cum animi ui* (I.159), with its elision of the first (stressed) syllable of **an**imi:

| quae c(um) anim- | -i ui

Less exceptionally, Augustan Latin poets (including Virgil) could and did sometimes break away from the Adonic to introduce spondees into the fifth foot – the *Aeneid* has lines ending with **com***itatu* and **ul***ulatu.* Lucretius has many more such 'heavy' four-syllabled words: examples include **sub***sidendo,* **perturben***tur,* **obbrutes***cat* and **susten***tare* – though he was, we should remember, struggling to express some pretty knotty technical issues in verse form. But these are the kind of thing that later poets generally avoided – let us take, by way of a *Sortes Nasonianae,* the regular Adonic endings of the first four lines of the *Metamorphoses*:

    i.   **di***cere* |***for***mas
    ii.   *(mu-)* | *-***tas***tis et* |*i***llas*
    iii. *(or-)* |*-***igi***ne* |***mun***di
    iv. **tem***pora* |***car***men

Easy to see why Ovid is the textbook darling of metrical correctness. But to conclude with one more exceptional modern example from the work of Professor Joseph Tusiani whose unique ear for the musicality of Latin can produce a line like this:

    fulgere oh pergat super umbras, umbras, umbras

Repetition of three remarkable heavy spondees in a row is something you won't find in Ovid!

So what about some advice for actual composition? Generally speaking the Adonic has proved to be so satisfying a termination that you will doubtless find yourself actively wanting to use it *most* of the time – which means in practice that you will be looking for patterns to match the *dum-diddy dum-dum* rhythm, ensuring that word stress falls on the first beat of both fifth and sixth feet and frequently concluding each line with a two-syllabled (stress on first syllable) or three-syllabled (stress on second syllable) word. The knock-on effect of which will make you (like Virgil above) want to avoid the coincidence of stress accent and metre in the third and certainly the fourth feet.

Just as Baroque composers like Vivaldi and Handel finished a musical phrase with *dum-di, dum-di daaaah,* or a guitarist like Eric Clapton throws in that distinctive run at the end of a 12-bar blues, the Adonic is the ideal way to round off your line. Exceptions both in Classical and Neo-Latin verse demonstrate that it's not a hard-and-fast rule; it is rather a useful ready-made weapon in your compositional arsenal.

- More technical analysis can be found in D.S. Raven's *Latin Metre* (Faber & Faber, 1965) Sections #69-76
- G.B Nussbaum's *Vergil's Metre* (Bristol Classical Press, 1986) has some excellent guidance on word accent and rhythm

       *   *   *

(4) Ex Libris: Some Books for Beginners

Piously we should always maintain that the very best way to learn how to write poetry is *to read* as much poetry as possible. But sometimes we need a bit of solid theoretical advice, too. So alongside your well-thumbed editions of Virgil, Catullus and Horace *et al.*, here is a suggested library of reference works to assist your poetical muse.

(1) *Dictionaries and the Gradus*

> *Oxford Latin Dictionary*, ed. P.G.W. Glare: OUP
>
> *Lewis & Short's Latin Dictionary*, ed. C.T. Lewis and C. Short: OUP
>
> *Cassell's Standard* or *Concise Latin-English, English-Latin Dictionary*, ed. D.P. Simpson: Casell.
>
> *Pocket Oxford* or *Oxford Desk Latin-English, English-Latin Dictionary*, ed. J. Morwood: OUP
>
> *Dictionary of Ecclesiastical Latin* (1995), ed. L.F. Stelton: Hendrickson Publishers.
>
> *Gradus ad Parnassum*, (aka 'Carey's Gradus'), various 19th and early-20th century editions.

The best (that is, most up-to-date, most authoritative) dictionary for Classical Latin is the massive *Oxford Latin Dictionary*. You will, however, need to hunt further afield for later Latin words – anything, that is, from roughly the third century onwards. For ecclesiastical and a certain amount of medieval Latin, the *Dictionary of Ecclesiatical Latin* is a useful supplement to the OLD. Alternatively, the 19th-century *Lewis & Short* does include later Latin – which is one good reason not to throw your old copy away when you acquire the new OLD. Both *Cassell's* and the *Pocket Oxford* (also available in hardback as a 'desk' edition) have an English-Latin section at the back, useful for both prose and poetry.

There is only one Latin thesaurus: the famous *Gradus ad Parnassum*, which is available in various editions – the nineteenth-century British version is often advertised by antiquarian booksellers as *Carey's Gradus*, from the edition best known to generations of Victorian and Edwardian schoolboys. In an ideal world, there would be a new, up-to-date *Gradus* to go alongside the big OLD. For the time being, however, we must content ourselves with tracking down old copies or finding an e-copy online.

(2) *Writing Latin Prose*

> Mountford, J.F. (ed.), *'Bradley's Arnold' Latin Prose Composition*, Bristol Classsical Press reissue (1998).
>
> R. Ashdowne, R. and J. Morwood (2007), *Writing Latin*, Bristol Classical Press.
>
> Minkova, M. (2001), *An Introduction to Latin Prose Composition* (2001), WPC Classics.
>
> Minkova, M. and Tunberg, T. (2004), *Readings and Exercises in Latin Prose Composition*, Focus Publishing.

Before embarking on verse, it might be a good idea to try some Latin prose writing. One old warhorse still in print today is the so-called 'Bradley's Arnold', a detailed and comprehensive prose manual that will certainly help hone your Caesarian despatches from the front line, though may be of less value if you actually want to write Latin about something of relevance to your own life. Richard Ashdowne and James Morwood's 2007 *Writing Latin* is more user-friendly. More radical is Milena Minkova and Terence Tunberg's *Readings and Exercises in Latin Prose Composition*, which actively encourages 'free' writing rather than simply translating set sentences: this is intended to be used in conjunction with Minkova's somewhat jargon-filled *Introduction to Latin Prose Composition*.

(3) *Writing Latin Verse*

Raven, D.S. (1965), *Latin Metre: An Introduction*, Faber and Faber.

Allen, W.S. (1965, rev. 1978), *Vox Latina: The Pronunciation of Classical Latin*, Cambridge University Press.

Califf, D.J. (2002), *A Guide to Latin Metre and Verse Composition*, Anthem Press.

Norberg, D. (1958, trans. 2004), *An Introduction to the Study of Medieval Latin Versification*, trans. G. C. Roti and J. de la Chapelle Skubly, Catholic University of America Press.

Brooks, C. (2007), *Reading Latin Poetry Aloud: A Practical Guide to Two Thousand Years of Verse*, Cambridge University Press.

D.S. Raven's 1965 manual *Latin Metre* remains as good an introduction as any to the varieties of classical verse forms. W.S. Allen's *Vox Latina* analyses Latin pronunciation and has much of value to say about word stress and the distinction between vowels (long or short) and syllable quantity (heavy or light). David Califf's 2002 *Guide to Latin Metre and Verse Composition* provides an abundance of practice exercises.

For anyone interested in the principles of medieval verse, including rhythmic or accentual verse, then Dag Norberg's 1958 *Introduction to the Study of Medieval Latin Versification* is indispensable.

A handy anthology of classical, medieval and neo-Latin verse is Clive Brooks' *Reading Latin Poetry Aloud*, which gives phonetic transcriptions alongside the Latin and English translations (and comes with two CDs of Brooks' rather deadpan recitations). The book also contains extremely helpful discussions of reading aloud, pronunciation and prosody.

(4) *Online Resources*

Just a couple of places to begin reading about this subject are:

Do-It-Yourself: How to Write Latin Verse (Harry C. Schnur)
http://www.suberic.net/~marc/schnur.html

Inter Versiculos (inspired by an 8-day workshop in Latin verse composition):
http://www.umich.edu/~rclatin/iv/index.html

And of course ....

Vates: The Journal of New Latin Poetry
http://pineapplepubs.snazzystuff.co.uk/vates.htm

*　　*　　*

Index of Poems by Title